MW00469489

Praise for
Untangled

"With tender, searing honesty, Koshin Paley Ellison shows us how to find peace and inner freedom right in the heart of our struggles and pain. The writing is heartfelt and charming, there's a fresh retelling of the Buddha's wisdom, and each page shines with insightful suggestions for a life that is brave, honest, and filled with love. I've never read a more compelling, liberating book."

—Rick Hanson, Ph.D., author of *Buddha's Brain,*
Hardwiring Happiness, Resilient, and
Making Great Relationships

"*Untangled* is a love letter to the broken-hearted. It is a balm for what ails us. Koshin Paley Ellison writes with the wit, wisdom, and loving embrace of one who has walked the path of heartache and loss and discovered the comfort of our shared humanity embedded in that experience. Each of us can be nourished by his words; each of us needs to be untangled so that we may live well and love each other. This is the book the world needs now."

—Jerry Colonna, author of
Reboot: Leadership and the Art of Growing Up.

"In Koshin Paley Ellison's wonderful book *Untangled*, he places the classical framework of the Buddha's Noble Eightfold Path in the context and complexity of our daily lives. The clarity of his open heart and deep wisdom shine on every page."

—Joseph Goldstein, author of
Mindfulness: A Practical Guide to Awakening

"This wonderful, thoroughly contemporary, totally engaging presentation of Buddhist wisdom uses sources as diverse as the Buddha and Dogen and Cinderella and Einstein and *Star Wars* and the author's grandmother, echoing the instruction that the Buddha gave to monks whom he had trained as they left his community to become teachers themselves: 'Teach the holy Dharma in the idiom of the people.' Koshin has done that! And I love it! It is a pleasure to read."

—Sylvia Boorstein, author of *Happiness Is an Inside Job*

"What!?? An approachable Zen Master? Who's willing to be vulnerable and is comfortable with hugs and tears? In *Untangled*, Koshin Paley Ellison reveals just such a Zen Master. In effortless prose full of personal stories and simple exercises, he offers a way for anyone who is willing to practice the Buddha's path of healing and transformation."

—Norman Fischer, Zen priest and author of
*When You Greet Me I Bow: Notes and
Reflections from a Life in Zen*

"Koshin Paley Ellison pays as much attention to inner practice as he does outer life. Here is a guide who approaches you with respect. Here is a friend on the page."

—Padraig O'Tauma, author of *Poetry Unbound*

"Personal, practical, intimate, and illuminating. *Untangled* is filled with vivid stories that give the practitioner much to think about and even more to feel."

—Laurie Anderson, avant-garde artist,
composer, musician, and film director

"Sadly, many of us get 'tangled' by the reality of everyday life, which for many results in suffering. In this wonderful book, we are given the opportunity to get 'untangled,' allowing for greater clarity and insight to not only understand the meaning of being present but, ultimately, our purpose in life."

—James R. Doty, M.D., founder and director of the
Stanford University Center for Compassion and
Altruism Research and Education (CCARE)

"Koshin's book *Untangled* guides us to find peace using Buddhist teachings. Koshin is a role model for Buddhist monks."

—Kodo Nishimura, makeup artist,
Buddhist monk, and LGBTQ activist

"Koshin Paley Ellison engages us from a life of hard-earned wisdom, showing us a way out of our countless tangles toward a path to freedom."

—Daniel Goleman, author of *Emotional Intelligence*

Untangled

Walking the Eightfold Path to
Clarity, Courage, and Compassion

KOSHIN PALEY ELLISON

balance

NEW YORK

Copyright © 2022 by Koshin Paley Ellison

Cover copyright © 2022 by Hachette Book Group, Inc.

Hachette Book Group supports the right to free expression and the value of copyright. The purpose of copyright is to encourage writers and artists to produce the creative works that enrich our culture.

The scanning, uploading, and distribution of this book without permission is a theft of the author's intellectual property. If you would like permission to use material from the book (other than for review purposes), please contact permissions@hbgusa.com. Thank you for your support of the author's rights.

Balance
Hachette Book Group
1290 Avenue of the Americas, New York, NY 10104
grandcentralpublishing.com
twitter.com/grandcentralpub

First Edition: November 2022

Balance is an imprint of Grand Central Publishing. The Balance name and logo is a trademark of Hachette Book Group, Inc.

The publisher is not responsible for websites (or their content) that are not owned by the publisher.

The Hachette Speakers Bureau provides a wide range of authors for speaking events. To find out more, go to www.hachettespeakersbureau.com or call (866) 376-6591.

Library of Congress Cataloging-in-Publication Data
Names: Paley Ellison, Koshin, author.
Title: Untangled : walking the eightfold path to clarity, courage, and compassion / by Koshin Paley Ellison.
Description: New York : Balance, 2022.
Identifiers: LCCN 2022019633 | ISBN 9781538708309 (hardcover) | ISBN 9781538708323 (ebook)
Subjects: LCSH: Eightfold Path. | Buddhism—Doctrines.
Classification: LCC BQ4320 .P35 2022 | DDC 294.3/42—dc23/eng/20220609
LC record available at https://lccn.loc.gov/2022019633

ISBNs: 978-1-5387-0830-9 (hardcover), 978-1-5387-0832-3 (ebook)

Printed in the United States of America

LSC-C

Printing 1, 2022

For my uncle Victor Honigmann, who was the first person I heard speak openly of terror and trauma as the gate to walk through toward healing and love.

Contents

The inner tangle and the outer tangle
This generation is entangled in a tangle.
And so I ask of Gotama this question:
Who succeeds in disentangling this tangle?

—*SAMYUTTA NIKAYA*

Truly, is anything missing now?

—HAKUIN EKAKU ZENJI (1686–1769)

PART I

BEFORE YOUR JOURNEY (IS THERE A BEFORE?)

Caminante, no hay camino, se hace camino al ander.
(Traveler, there is no path to follow, you make your own
way as you walk.)

—ANTONIO MACHADO

CHAPTER 1

True Pleasure Is a Place of Practice

When I was eight years old, I told my mother that I wanted to grow up to be a Zen Buddhist monk. Today I am a Zen monk dedicated to serving my Zen students and training people in contemplative approaches to care and medicine. All the time I work with dying people, and only a few of them know they are dying. I am also a sensual person. I have always loved to feel the warmth of the sun on my arm, run my fingers through the grass, or notice the light flickering through the autumn leaves. As a child, I loved to watch the beauty of the clouds moving over the treetops. As a poet friend of mine likes to say, I was "ravaged by beauty." It shook me up.

I enjoyed these pleasures of the body, yet my experience of the body was also indelibly marked by growing up in a home that held violence and fear: an unstable, unpredictable home. I was raised by loving, ethically idealistic people with, at times, a huge gap between that and how they actually functioned in the world. At a very young age I learned that my body could end. One of the people who lived in my house would often go into rages. You could hear their voice rising, but the scariest sound was the knife drawer opening and the screaming after that, without knowing exactly what was going on from where I was curled up inside the locked upstairs bathroom. I wish I could tell you more details of what happened. I can tell you my body was on high alert. I felt the lack of safety and was keenly aware that this body—my body—was in danger.

This feeling was reinforced through other experiences of violence. In my middle school years, while waiting at the bus stop, I would often find myself alone with the school bully. I was very small, and so I was a favorite target to push down on the ground, the contents of my book bag thrown all over the place in the snow and gravel. Before school, after school, it was all the same shtick, liberally sprinkled with name-calling: *fag* and *queer* and so on. Often, I would see blood and life become clear: This is real, this vulnerable body bleeding. Inside the house that could happen; outside the house that could happen. It felt like there was no way out.

Then a small escape opened up. The summer that *Star Wars* came out, in 1977, I started biking to the mall. It was so amazing! My friend Jason and I would ride our bikes to the mall again and again to see it. I loved Luke Skywalker, who was so whiny and so annoying, which was how I saw myself. Luke was also trapped in a condition that he didn't like or choose. His body was locked in place, which I related to. Like me, he and his family lived in a spiritual hole, in a spiritually—and actually—barren place. His parents were not his parents, which I also related to. I was sure that something happened to my parents that caused them to disconnect their actions from their core values. They both allowed for the suffering of violence to continue in our houses after their divorce.

Yet it was through this same circumstance that Luke ended up meeting his teacher, Obi-Wan Kenobi, through those particular difficult causes and conditions, and that blew my mind. Could something like that happen to me? Could I find a teacher? None of the teachers at school felt like a teacher to me—or *for* me—and it was then that I started to understand it was possible to actually learn from someone; a person could take you under their wing and help you to leave your hole. *Star Wars* introduced me to the idea of a student-teacher relationship. I realized that was what I wanted, and soon life pointed toward where it might be found.

At home, no one knew how to get out of this painful gap; everyone seemed trapped, tussling around in our metaphorical hole with our bodies and minds hurting or getting hurt. I wanted to find life beyond that. Then once again I was saved by a movie: *The Karate Kid* came out. There it was again—a teacher and a whiny, annoying kid, which is how I continued to see myself. I thought maybe karate could be the way out, and I learned that there was a dojo in a local strip mall near our house. It was in a basement, and it was mildewy in there, just like the swamp on Degobah. The teacher, Sensei White, used to make us sit in seiza with our knees tucked under our bodies. It turned out that he was a Zen guy. "You'll never be free until you can be still with your pain," he said. That teaching remains essential for me to this day.

I realized that the people in my house were flailing around from their pain and couldn't seem to stop moving. There was no stillness, no reflection, and they were hurting people and themselves. Sitting on a wood floor with your knees underneath your body is really painful. For me, learning to be with that pain was key. I was sitting there, sweating in seiza, and I felt like I was learning a superpower. It felt like this was actually what I needed to learn in order to experience real freedom. I needed to learn how to be still. This was the beginning, for me, of moving from being driven by my pain to finding a way to be in skillful relationship with it. It was the beginning of a shift from being a victim of my life toward seeing my life as a place of practice.

TANGLES OF OUR OWN MAKING

The suffering we feel is rooted in how tangled up we are. Many of us feel tangled by our fears, our resentments, and our stories about ourselves and others. We feel controlled by behaviors we can't change, thoughts we can't stop, feelings we don't want to feel. We feel tangled in confusion, or in misperception, or in traumas we haven't learned how to heal. Living so tangled up contorts our bodies, and we end up walking through life like "the ministry of silly walks" in the old Monty Python skit. This reduces our avail-ability to life, to others, and to our true selves.

In the early texts of Buddhism, someone is said to have approached the Buddha (whose name was Siddhartha Gotama) and asked, "The inner tangle and the outer tangle, this generation is entangled in a tangle. And so I ask of Gotama this question: Who succeeds in disentangling this tangle?" It is up to you and me to untangle it.

The "tangle" is all the ways we bind ourselves up in our fears, our unhelpful stories, and our self-created clouds of confusion. It is made out of the ways we try to seek happiness and avoid suf-fering that totally don't work. I've experienced it myself, and I see it often with the students who study with me. No matter the differences in where they're from, how they look, or what they do, the students who come to me so often feel overwhelmed, stress, anxiety, and loneliness. They suffer from a profound disconnect from others, like they're floating in space, untethered. They often—sometimes very often—think that their actual experiences or even their entire lives are not as good as ones they've idealized. They are consumed by the fear that they are unlovable just as they are. The suspicion, often unnamed but still lurking under the surface of everything, is that they'll never be enough to meet what life brings their way.

The experience of the COVID-19 pandemic heightened a lot of this suffering. Certainly, in the United States, as loved ones became ill, many people died, employment became precarious, and our daily behavior was strictly limited, feelings of instability and fear of disaster came rushing to the fore. The virus exacerbated the anxiety that is threaded through a lot of economic, political, and social issues. Our vulnerability was exposed, and we were reminded that we are not in control. Suddenly, our fragility felt very real.

Life is fragile. It's delicate and subject to ever-changing circumstances. The epidemic didn't create that reality; it only made it clearer. We try to hide the tangles we're caught in under fancy clothes. We pretend that the lopsided way we're walking through life is a swagger. What happens when the costumes and coping mechanisms are pulled away? Among the many extraordinary things about the entire world going through the shared traumas of COVID-19 was that it made our shared suffering more visible.

The Loneliness Epidemic

A physician I know is consumed with the feeling that they are never meeting expectations. They didn't reach everyone they wanted to reach that day. They didn't do everything they could have done. If you were to meet this person, you would see that everything about them radiates warmth. Their body language is open. Their smiles are wide. Judging by outer appearances, you'd think they are free of storms and struggles. In actuality, the whole of their professional life has been plagued by feelings of inadequacy, born from a deeply held and unexamined delusion that they should have no bounds.

So many of us hold fast to an anxious belief that we must do some particular thing or be some particular way in order to be lovable. We can become so fixated on this seemingly urgent requirement that all we see is our own success and (inevitable) failure instead of the real people we are supposed to be loving and being loved by. Ultimately we are incapable of enjoying the simple giving and taking that our strategy was meant to bring us. This is one of many different tangles that can ensnare us in self-referential obsessions even as we wonder why we are so exhausted, so frustrated, and so lonely.

Loneliness is itself a different kind of public health epidemic. Hundreds of articles have been published about loneliness and its detrimental effects on our mental, emotional, and physical health. Britain has even appointed a loneliness minister. Their role is to address the erosion of families and communities, the tearing apart of the social fabric, rising divorce rates, and all forms of isolation. And yet, on a daily basis, how many people do you personally see or hear expressing that they're unbearably lonely? One of the symptoms of the trouble is that the ones suffering from loneliness often do not share their struggle—sometimes they don't know how to name it even for themselves.

Junk Pleasure

The consequences of the way we tangle ourselves up are very real. Even those of us who have succeeded in ways that society values—getting married, making money, acquiring status—often feel unanchored, disengaged, and empty, and they can't figure out why. Frequently, we attempt to fill the hole we feel with junk pleasure, which our culture feeds us in steady supply: shopping, alcohol and drugs, sex and porn, food, you name it. It's not that there's anything wrong with these things in and of themselves (personally, I've got a weakness for Apple products). It's that they aren't able to do what we're asking them to do. And when they fail or are not available, then we can get desperate.

During the COVID-19 pandemic we have been told many times that what we need to do is "shelter in place." This has often sounded to me like a coded message from the universe, a Zen message, if you will, because amid our pain, sheltering in place is exactly what we need to do. We need to take shelter in being exactly in the place that we are now, because when we do that, where we are now becomes the place of practice.

Finding Shelter Is a Place of Practice

The following is a practice to help you begin to identify your tangles. It's a good way to begin working with the practices in this book, and you can return to it any time.

Find somewhere to sit comfortably. Let your body settle in a way that feels good. Make whatever microadjustments are needed. Be aware of your breathing, and then let your awareness of your breath draw you into your lower belly. Allow your belly to be soft. Let your awareness arrive fully in the body, flowing throughout it until you can feel the sensations throughout your body. Feel clearly that your body is your place. This body of sensations right here, with its tension and pleasures, its tingling and its vibrations, this body of sensations is your home. Let the sensations rise freely into your awareness. Let yourself settle as one with them. Let them hold your awareness, anchoring it and giving your mind a place to shelter.

Entering a place of refuge is a place of practice.

SHEDDING THE THREADS

By the time students come to me, they've often tried many different things to make themselves happy, and none of them have worked. They've come to the hard-won, dispiriting realization that the things that seem so pleasurable are not, really. What they thought would satisfy them doesn't last. They don't feel like society has given them any real answers. Sometimes they're at their absolute wit's end. What they're after is nothing short of a truly happy life, one free from the hold of junk pleasure that satisfies our urge for instant gratification but does not provide true nourishment. They're tired of living all tangled up, and yet they have no idea how to get out of it alone.

This is the same plight that a certain guy you may have heard of found himself struggling with a long time ago in India. He led a privileged life and yet was confronted by some grim realities: that everything changes and we get old and sick and die. He was a prince, so all the luxuries of an actual palace stopped being of interest to him. Once those truths sunk in, the distractions he was used to were no longer of interest to him. Shaken by the realization, he set out to transform his life.

As important a figure as the Buddha was and is, I think about him as just another person continuously practicing. What he did was take an honest account of our situation as human beings—all of our vulnerabilities and the way we cause ourselves needless suffering—then, as the texts tell it, he vowed to never again build himself a house of sorrow. It's the poetic way of saying that he looked around and thought, "Damn! I've got to see through all my bullshit."

Wanting to get your shit together is a powerful and important place to be. It's the beginning of deep inquiry. Inquiry is central to transforming our awareness. Many spiritual traditions have lineages, much like family trees. Inquiry is so fundamental to the view of practice in my own Soto Zen lineage that an ancestor in my lineage, Hongzhi Zhengjue, used a Chinese phrase meaning "inquiry" to sum up the whole of Buddhist practice. From that place of readiness to inquire deeply, we can start to answer the simplest and most complex question that we face as human beings: What is my life about, and how do I live my values in it?

What's interesting is that for many of us, the shape of the answer is the same, just as the biggest, heaviest threads in our tangle are the same. What we want is a life infused with meaning, marked by genuine connection, and aligned with what matters most. A life like that is full of true pleasure. True pleasure is the other side of junk pleasure; it can't be produced through any of the means we're used to. This type of life builds gradually, but with a more solid foundation—it can't be swept away by circumstance or anyone else, because the only thing it depends on is you. It takes a big effort to cultivate, but is 100 percent possible. And it's totally free.

When you figure out how to keep growing true pleasure, it pervades your life inside and out. That's a good thing not only for you, but for others, too. An untangled person isn't spending a lot of time struggling to move and walk without pain. With freedom of movement and true pleasure comes a feeling of richness, maybe for the first time. Richness enables generosity. In a time of ecological crisis, rising inequality, violence, and trauma, surely the world needs our generosity. It needs people who feel rich enough to give, which has nothing to do with your bank account.

Stepping on the Eightfold Path

Fortunately, the Buddha not only figured out how to see through his shit; he also taught others how to do it. That's the original definition of a Buddha—someone who both wakes themselves up and is able to teach others how to wake themselves up too. The method he laid out for cultivating a life of true pleasure is called the Eightfold Path. The Eightfold Path is a place of practice, a container for our aspirations and longings for freedom that can carry us to our true home.

The eight parts of the path are a time-tested map for transformation that people have been following for almost three thousand years. Making the Eightfold Path our place of practice catalyzes inner change that radiates into our external lives, from everyday interactions to our most intimate relationships. The true pleasure it creates is one that calms us, grounds us, and sustains us, making the bad times more easily borne and the good times even better.

I've spent the last thirty-five years of my life practicing the Eightfold Path. When you make a home in it, it makes a home in you. It turned me from someone who was traumatized and untrusting into someone I never thought I'd be: joyful, open, and able to reflect that energy back into the world.

Picture the eight aspects of the path like eight spokes on a wheel leading into the central hub. That central hub is where we find true pleasure, which is the joy of the path. Anywhere on the wheel is walkable, including all the roads, the outer rim, and the central hub. There is no arrival point or finish line, although you can spend more and more time within the hub of true pleasure.

The Eightfold Path won't help you strike it rich, lose weight, or win friends and influence people. What these practices will do is help you untangle, and when you do that, you'll be free to stretch your wings. Heck, you'll be free to howl at the moon. This is the freedom that would appear if you forgave who you are and expressed your true nature—if you let your freak flag fly.

Don't Hold Back

I believe that everyone intuits there is a way to live that is easeful, connected, authentic, and free. Most of us have had moments, or even seasons of life, when we felt like that. Some people have the idea that it's a kind of heaven, and that it can't exist in this world. The design perspective, so to speak, of Buddhism is different. Freedom exists here, where we are, moment by moment, and this can be invited and cultivated. Living a life of true pleasure is living with a sense of expansion, of exploration and curiosity, of having wild access to the full range of human experience from the depths of the Pacific Ocean to the heights of Everest. Learning how to live like this requires what is required of all adventurers: courage. It's the courage to say what you value and stick to it. It's the courage to stop fucking around, because life is short.

Fifteen years ago, my husband, Chodo, and I had the honor of care partnering with a woman named Rose as she was dying. I think about her when I think about courage.

"Promise me you won't hold back," she said to us, on her deathbed. Her energy had been low and quiet for days, but she became exuberant for a minute while she spoke. "I held back for twenty years," she said. "Then I didn't anymore, and I have no regrets. Promise me you won't hold back."

This is the kind of courage we need to walk the eight roads and create a life of true pleasure. Ready? Don't worry—you never will be. Let's begin anyway.

Out of suffering have emerged the strongest souls; the most massive characters are seared with scars.

—KAHLIL GIBRAN

Buddha is a statue of liberty, a symbol of interdependence and freedom. When you see the Buddha statue, do not ask for a solution or to be free from problems, because our problems are the things that nobody else can solve. Even the Buddha cannot solve the problem. He teaches us how to be with this problem. So when you see the Buddha statue, do not ask for solutions. Ask to struggle together. Please struggle together with me.

—GENYU KOJIMA ROSHI

CHAPTER 2

The Tangle

Before we begin exploring the Eightfold Path, we should become familiar with what is blocking us from walking it. What are the tangles that are constricting our arms and legs so we can't move, or covering our mouths so we can't speak? We won't end our suffering unless we understand it first. So, we begin by focusing on our suffering itself, so that once understood, it can become malleable and workable.

As we age, the jolts and injuries of life can add up and gradually become active in us as forces that take away our autonomy and our presence. Instead of our life being a place of practice, it becomes a place of escaping, a place where we try to run from ourselves. That is, of course, impossible, so our lives become places of impossibility instead of places of possibility.

Opening the Cage

The following practice can help open you up to the possibility of going beyond your stories. Before we can be free, we often need to be able to imagine ourselves free.

Imagine yourself locked in a tight cage almost the same shape as your body. Feel how uncomfortable it is—the lack of movement and possibilities. The bars of the cage are made out of your stories that limit you. What stories are the bars in front of you made out of? For me, these are the stories I tell myself most often—the greatest hits. Then, imagine the stories that make up the side walls of your cage. What are the stories you are less conscious of that squeeze you in? Breathe into them. How does that feel? Now take a moment to imagine the bars behind you. What are the stories that keep you against the wall? Breathe into these. Now, imagine that the cage is unlocked, as it actually has always been. What does that feel like in your body and mind? As you push the door open, what happens?

Unlocking our cages is a place of practice.

SOFTENING YOUR NARRATIVE

In my life, I've struggled with the narrative that I am a victim, a story I inherited from hearing my family talk about the Holocaust. My great-uncle was imprisoned in a concentration camp; my grandparents would often talk about their extended family being killed for who they were. My grandpa George used to hold up a book called *The Indestructible Jews* and say, "Remember this! We will always be victimized." I think it's interesting how he overlooked the other implication of the title. I was getting consistent messages from a very early age that the Jews were a vulnerable, endangered people, and so that must have meant that I was endangered too.

On top of that, I experienced sexual, physical, and emotional violence in my family. This fed the narrative I was constructing: Not only were other people going to harm me, but the people who said they loved me were going to harm me too. At school, I was being bullied for being gay. I felt like there was danger everywhere I went.

As a teenager and into adulthood, this resulted in a deep, unmet longing for, and fear of, connection. I was so lost and had such little understanding of who I was that I made all my decisions based on fear and a preconceived notion of my identity as someone who was preyed upon. This is how I ended up, for instance, in my freshman year of college thinking that joining a fraternity would make me feel a sense of belonging in the new, unsafe environment of college. Since what I was becoming was an out gay man, it made me feel the total opposite (although I did meet some lifelong friends in my fraternity).

These are just some examples of how we let our tangles shape our lives. We look up through all the layers of our past suffering, and then make matters worse for ourselves. This is how a gay Jewish man becomes vice president of a heteronormative fraternity, or how people can reach the end of their lives and not feel like they've lived at all.

Rather than simply repeating the same mistakes over and over, we have to learn how to direct our thoughts and then our actions differently. We can do this by finding shelter in our place of practice and acting from there. This is the underlying principle of walking the Eightfold Path.

GETTING BEYOND AND
GETTING INTIMATE

Walking the Eightfold Path means balancing two principles: becoming intimate with our suffering and exploring what else is true. In order to balance, it helps to walk this together, shoulder to shoulder. I invite you to do this together with me here.

Getting Intimate

Zen Centers around the world perform a ceremony called the Gate of Sweet Nectar, which is an old Buddhist ceremony to feed what the tradition calls "hungry ghosts." Hungry ghosts were believed to be lost spirits who were wandering the cosmos, fixated on obsessions they couldn't let go of. You might be able to relate. Maybe think of this ceremony as compassionately feeding our inner demons with care to reduce their pain. There's a line at the end of a chant that goes, "May all evil be satisfied and be quieted by this effort." I know that the word *evil* has a lot of baggage. Here you can think of it as simply suffering, and quieting it as simply being in healthy relationship with that suffering—acknowledging that it's there and seeing what you can do about getting to know it. This point is crucial.

In the Gate of Sweet Nectar ceremony, the hungry ghosts are not banished or killed. They're being cared for like you'd quiet a small child having a tantrum. When walking the eight roads we'll describe in this book, this is the kind of kindness and patience with which we should approach our "evil." With this in mind, getting intimate means getting to know our suffering the best we can, since it's impossible to work with something that is only a mystery to us. It also means staying intimate with what we find there, even if it frightens us.

We all have a legion inside of us, like the possessed man in the Bible story. We're all capable of evil. As soon as you think you've successfully rid yourself of it, you're likely heading for disaster. When you know who your demons are and how they like to work, you can start figuring out how to quiet their tantrums by swaddling them with love.

Moving through Suffering

Getting beyond means not imprisoning yourself inside the stories you tell yourself about yourself. Who would you be, and what kind of life would you live, if you didn't believe you were only a certain way?

My husband, Chodo, began learning about getting beyond his stories from the first Buddhist he ever met. Back then he was Robert (Chodo is his Buddhist name). He had just gotten sober. He was taking care of his body, going through psychoanalytic training, and continuing to meet weekly with a supervisor. And yet he still felt empty inside.

At his weekly appointments he kept on seeing this interesting woman with piercing blue eyes and a bald head walking around the place. He mentioned to his supervisor how sad it was that this woman had cancer, and his supervisor laughed. "She doesn't have cancer," he said. "She's a Buddhist monk. You should go talk to her."

The next time he saw the woman, Chodo cornered her in the hallway and said practically all in one breath, "Hi, my name is

Robert, and I'm really interested in learning from you. I'm an alcoholic and a former drug addict…" He went on and on and on—he
was talking nonstop, word-vomiting all over the poor woman. He
thought it was so important to share his narratives about who he was,
because through them was how he engaged with the world.

When he was finally done, the woman responded, "Well, you
know what you need to do."

"No, I don't," Chodo said. "Tell me."

"You need to shut the fuck up."

In the Zen tradition we don't mince words. "Shut the fuck up"
can be pretty good advice when we are loving and clear. To walk
the Eightfold Path, first we need to learn how to stop and give
ourselves a break from the tape we're constantly playing. This can
be hard for anyone, but it can be especially hard if you've experienced a lot of trauma. To move into the space of getting beyond,
you need to have done a certain amount of healing first. Healing
goes together with being able to start looking at whether you're
holding on to past suffering that you don't need to hold on to anymore. I know we can feel almost addicted to our life's stories, even
sad or ugly ones. Victimhood, for instance, can easily be turned
into a type of self-absorption that we don't want to let go of; it's
that feeling of "nobody knows the trouble I've seen." You're ready
to practice with getting beyond when you're tired of living from
within that prison, which is actually a way to avoid getting hurt by
others.

Bringing "getting beyond" and "getting intimate" into equa-
nimity requires a lot of skill. Sometimes that means bringing gentle energy to the task, and sometimes that means coming at it with
the force of a jackhammer. Sometimes it means letting wounds

heal for a while on their own in the darkness of our being without shining a bright light on them at the wrong time. It's knowing when it is the right moment to push ahead and when it is the right moment to rest. Keep that in mind as we start to talk about our personal suffering in the chapters to come.

Getting Intimate, Getting Beyond

We cannot choose our bodies, race, ethnicity, gender, sexuality, personalities, or brain chemistry. We cannot choose our histories. We are these things, yet we are more than them too. When we are truly intimate with them—which means experiencing them just as they are—then we live beyond them as well. Sound like a paradox? It is. As Shunryu Suzuki said, "If it's not paradoxical, it's not true."

Begin by taking a comfortable sitting posture. Let your awareness spread gently through your body, and become aware of your breath. Feel the sensations of sitting and breathing, and let whatever other sensations arise in the body come into your awareness and move through it freely. Relax around the sensations of body and breath. Let things be.

Can you feel how soothing it is to give the mind a home within the body? Can you feel how soothing it is to the body to be gifted the loving attention of awareness? When body and mind are together like this, this is intimacy.

Keep on relaxing into your body and breath, letting the self settle into the self. When we are intimate with body and mind, unafraid, holding them with our gentle attention, we are free. Paradoxically, we are not bowled over by emotions or thoughts or feelings. We are beyond them as we use our very freedom to embrace them.

Meditation is a place of practice.

BEGINNING IN THE BODY

While the particular nuances of everyone's suffering are different, the general contours are universal. Because of that, we can walk the path of practice together, learning from one another. We tend to tangle ourselves up in our physical bodies, our feelings, and the ways that we think, so these are our first places of practice.

My dream is that people will find a way back home, into their bodies, to connect with the earth, to connect with each other, to connect with the poor, to connect with the broken, to connect with the needy, to connect with people calling out all around us, to connect with the beauty, poetry, the wildness.

—V (FORMERLY EVE ENSLER)

PART II

BEGINNING TO GO
BEYOND

Where you stand, where you are, that's what your life is right there, regardless of how painful it is or how enjoyable it is. That's what it is.

—TAIZAN MAEZUMI ROSHI

CHAPTER 3

You Are Not Just Your Body

One day I learned a simple but profound lesson about bodies. The red Schwinn bike I had for years had brake pedals instead of hand brakes. One day I took my stepsister's bike out for a ride. It was much bigger and had hand brakes. I was zooming down a hill really fast. The cars were coming up at me, and I got disoriented and frightened. I heard someone shout, "Pull the brakes on the handlebars!" I did, and I went flying off the bike. Somehow, I ended up flat on my face, right underneath this woman's car. My front teeth are still chipped!

I remember sitting up and seeing the blood all over my body. I was shaking uncontrollably. This woman was getting out of the car—which I had been underneath—and was clearly in shock herself. She came up and put her arm around me—I can still feel it. It was so ordinary. It was a vulnerable body taking care of another vulnerable body, like we've been doing for tens of thousands of years.

Someone once asked the anthropologist Margaret Mead what the first sign of civilization is. She said that it's finding a skeleton with a femur bone that was broken and healed. Why is that? It's because in premodern conditions you couldn't survive with that kind of break without other people helping you. That day, when I fell off the bike, that woman's intervention was so primal and timeless. Our deepest needs are so ordinary. This was tapping into what we've known for a long time as a species. It was her ordinary action that mattered, one body taking care of another body, walking me home. In the last chapter I said that being able to be still in the face of pain is one way to go beyond the suffering of our bodies. The ordinary care between people is another.

WHAT IS THE WAY?

By this time, I had been practicing karate for a while. As for the school bully, he was still doing what he was doing. At my karate dojo, Sensei White was telling me "Never use this to harm anyone" over and over again, and I was taking that seriously. One day the bully kept pushing and pushing, though, and each time I'd get up, he would knock me down again. After the fourth time something inside of me snapped. We were in front of his house—he was my neighbor—and I said, "You can't do that to me anymore." I was small and effeminate, and he was so surprised.

"What are you gonna do about it?" he asked.

I hauled off and landed a roundhouse kick to his head, and I said, "That." I still remember the sensation of my foot hitting his head and his whole body moving. I was immediately horrified: Somehow, I had become what I feared.

That didn't stop him. He got up and came at me, and, not to put too fine a point on it, I responded by beating him up. He began to cry, and I began to cry, and his mother opened the window and said, "What are you doing to my son?"

I said, "Your son is an asshole and you should take care of him." Let's just say that sometimes when we first start pushing back against the world, we can begin by pushing too hard.

The true horror of that incident, for me, was twofold. First, I was so ashamed of what I did that I never went back to the karate school that had become such a refuge for me. Second, the next day at school everyone knew what had happened. Suddenly I was walking down the hallway, the one that always felt scary to me, and everyone was giving me high fives that I had beat up the school bully, who had terrorized other students. I remember a sick feeling in my stomach and my body, and yet at the same time I felt excited. That mixture of sickening and exhilarating feelings made me deeply nervous. I couldn't reconcile what that meant.

That fight helped me to realize that I had to get out of the world of bodies hurting each other, where I seemed to be trapped. I began to intuit that I needed to untangle my pain, but I didn't know how. I knew that kicking bullies wasn't the way.

I learned from somewhere that you could miss twenty-five days of school and still graduate, so I learned how to forge my dad's signature well enough to write notes excusing myself and spent more time wandering by myself. I didn't know how to regulate my own body, and I didn't know what was happening to it, but I was looking for a way.

The Buddha said that this is where our quest starts—in suffering. It doesn't start there just once, let me tell you! It starts and restarts when we find that we've become trapped and tangled. The Buddha said words of encouragement, though, that from suffering comes search, and from search comes conviction. Conviction is born when something we hear, see, read, or think shifts our perspective and we glimpse a way out. Then we take the first step.

Thinking back on your own life, can you remember a time when suffering led you to a new way of living or a new insight?

BEYOND TO THE BENEATH

Several days a month, I would cross the golf course near our house and get behind it, where there was a beautiful quarry with big, wonderful stones. I would find large ones to lie on, preferably with moss on them, enjoying the feeling of support. Doing this made me feel like the earth could support me. I didn't know where else I could get that support. I needed something that was wild because my body felt wild. It felt confused, afraid, and excited, so I would go and not do much but imagine where I could be.

It was only through finding that sense of gravity I had learned from Sensei White, of really valuing stillness, that there began to be freedom. To this day I love looking up at the light and the trees like I would then. When you feel supported, you can open up and see the cracks in things where the light comes through. At times I drive Chodo a little crazy saying "Look at the light through the trees." Maybe a year ago, though, we were sharing an exercise about what we appreciate about each other, and he said, "I love that you're always pointing to the light through the trees." What he does not fully know is how the light through the trees, in many ways, saved me then. It was through that stillness which allowed observation. It was through that feeling of being held in my body by the earth that allowed me to look up and see the light filtering through from above.

When that woman put her arm around me when I crashed on my bike, I understood that my body was also my friend. Through those days lying still on the earth, that's how I began to learn to connect to the body of the world. That was another step on the way to freedom, the beginning of conviction. A few years later I met my first Zen teacher in Boulder, Colorado. I learned zazen—seated meditation—for the first time (see chapter 15), taught by the first man that I had ever seen wearing robes on the street. Zazen underneath a gum tree—we sat there together, and it felt like the true beginning of home, of refuge.

Many years later, I've dedicated my life to teaching people and companioning with them, walking shoulder to shoulder with them. We are learning how to be still in our bodies, how to support each other, and how to feel the support of the great earth and all beings in their interconnection, so that we can be free.

Meditation: Being Supported by the Earth

Find somewhere to sit comfortably. Let your body settle in a way that feels good. Make whatever microadjustments are needed. Be aware of your breathing, and then let your awareness of your breath draw you into your lower belly. Allow your belly to be soft. Let your awareness arrive fully in the body, flowing throughout it until you can feel the sensations throughout your body. Become aware of the earth beneath you. Feel how broad and expansive it is, and how it supports your whole life. Feel how with the earth beneath you there is nowhere to fall. Become aware that your whole body is made of the earth, as is your clothing and whatever else you have with you. As you breathe with awareness, be aware of how the earth holds your body. Feel this connection, that the earth is part of you, supporting your life.

Resting in gratitude is a place of practice.

WE ARE—AND ARE NOT—OUR BODIES

While I spend all my time with people who are dying, I spend some time each week with people who know they are dying. Almost all of the people who know they are dying wish they weren't—very few are okay with what's happening. A particular woman I spent time with had a very aggressive form of cancer and was being treated with heavy doses of steroids. Her cheeks were swallowing her face. She would cry and cry. She didn't want this to be happening. She taught me how to sit with her in her pain.

This woman was well loved, and many of her friends would come, a stream of people bringing cards and balloons—she was particularly fond of rabbits. People would encourage her, tell her "You're going to get better. You're going to fight this. It's going to work out. Fight harder." She told me—and it took her a long time to say things because her mouth was so squeezed—"I have done what I can do." I told her that I knew that.

She turned her head a little—it hurt her so much to move—and she pulled the folds from her face to reveal her nose and mouth, and she said, "You see me."

I'll never forget her hands literally pulling her face out, and she said, "And I want someone to see me clearly before I go." She said, "Because now you've seen me and I have seen you, now I can let go of this body."

The name of the woman in the hospital bed was Theresa. She died the next day. I was holding her hand. She left me a clay heart. She said, "It's beautiful and fragile. It reminds me of our bodies." We're attached, and we're grasping at what our bodies were, or to them being safe. When we remember how precious and also fragile the body is, though, we can appreciate it for the time we have it, which is not terribly long.

If half of the time I don't even know that I have a body, it is difficult to learn that we are more than just our bodies. I have a personal trainer—that's one of the ways I care for my body. While working out, I twisted my knee in a funky way. I got curious about the sharpness of the painful, pulsing, needlelike sensations. Walking down the street, I started noticing other people in a way that I had not noticed before. I started noticing people walking differently, with little twists of pain on their faces. I saw how people were walking around with their bodies in pain, and not just older people, but younger people with a little limp too, a little grimace when they were walking down the subway stairs. When everything in our bodies feels fine, we can blind ourselves to the realities of life, like we're walking around in a *Tom and Jerry* cartoon, where no one ever actually gets hurt. When we are hurting, though, we wake up to the fleeting, vulnerable nature of our life and the struggles of the people around us. In early Buddhism illness, aging, and death were called the *devadhutas*—the divine messengers. When we feel the fragility of our bodies, we can become so much more aware of our shared fragility. This can spur us to take up the path of compassion and community, and to take responsibility for our relationship to our own bodies. Sickness is a divine messenger.

Zen in the Body

What I need for my own body is attention. I need to learn how to slow down and actually feel into my own body. Lying on the floor and moving and getting curious and seeing what it needed—this was a way of getting really interested. One of my teachers used to say "interesting" comes from "to be between," which is so beautiful. I started getting into these spaces in my own body and slowly, over time, learned how to start working with my body differently so it could heal.

One way to care for the body is to learn how to pay attention to our posture. I'm embarrassed to say that for many years, even in seated meditation, I sat with terrible posture. A friend of mine who is a chiropractor as well as a Zen monk taught me how to hold my body so it could actually be a vessel for the development of my mind. They taught me to allow my hips to be forward so my back curves, how to allow my belly to be soft, my shoulders to open. How to hold my head up through the crown like they tell you in yoga, and slightly tuck my chin in, and how awkward that felt for quite some time.

One of the things I love about Zen is the uprightness in the body that we learn in our practices. Whether we are sitting in a chair or lying down on a cushion, we can still be upright in our bodies. I remember that about Bernie Glassman, the great Zen teacher—he was in his body, it was a little bit hunched, it was not the style of his body to look upright in a stereotypical way—but yet he could still be upright in his body. Being upright is not just a matter of a preconceived posture; it is deeper than that.

Why Me? Why Not Me?

When people receive difficult news, the most popular response is "why me?"—as if the body is betraying us instead of just following the reality of bodies, which is to be brilliant and amazing and vulnerable and temporary. Years ago, when I had surgery, the surgeon said to me, "There's a 99.9 percent chance this is nothing, so don't worry about it," and it turned out to be that 0.1 percent that was cancer. I remember feeling like the floor had dropped out from under me. I remember leaving his office, and right next to it was an iron gate. It was cold outside, and I put my hand on the iron gate and held the iron bar, feeling the cold of it. I took a long, slow exhale and said to myself, "My turn."

In many ways I feel my life had prepared me for that moment. My awareness of danger in my life, the temporariness of life in a body, how fragile it is. I can still feel that cold iron. I felt supported by it—like the great rocks in the quarry—by that sensation. I needed to come back to my body, to the concrete reality of it, in order to go beyond my pain and fear of losing my body and my life. Ultimately the cancer was removed through surgery, and my practice of attention and awareness through each moment prepared me to meet what the vulnerability of my body brought.

THE GATE

There's a gorgeous poem by Marie Howe in her book *What the Living Do*. In this poem, "The Gate," Howe reflects on her brother and how he had washed every glass and rinsed every plate under the cold tap, and how we will do that only a certain number of times. After my cancer diagnosis, I remember feeling that iron gate and realizing I can feel this I, here, now. That movement into appreciating this body for the time we have it.

For me, the challenge of true appreciation is realizing how fragile this body is. It hangs by a thread. Some people think that's depressing, but I have come to find it exhilarating. It makes me appreciate more and more what I'm actually experiencing with this body.

When I say we are not just the body, I am not saying we are not the body at all. The investigation into what it means to be this body is one of the great adventures of this life. Learning to care for the body, learning to listen to it, and learning how to be attuned to the body are pathways to realizing that we are not just our bodies. We can find freedom beyond the memories buried in our bodies, beyond what they have been through. We can find freedom in what happens between our bodies. We can find support in the body of the earth, which grounds and sustains all bodies. And when we come home to our bodies to take care of them, we can find that our bodies return the favor by becoming a teacher and a refuge for us.

Meditation on Receiving the Unwelcome

Imagine receiving news you feel is unwelcome. It could be emotional, physical, or spiritual news. It might be a disappointment, a doubt, a diagnosis. Notice what it does to your body and your mind. Where do you contract? Where do you open? Return to your breath and place your hands on your hara, that place in your body two inches below your belly button. Allow your breath to steady and flow. Feel how your breath moves your hands. Bring into your heart and mind the phrase "My turn." This is your opportunity to meet the unwelcome as a teacher. What does welcoming the unwelcome do to you? Stay with your breath in your hara, letting it move your hands. This is your turn to meet what you feel you can't meet with love.

Turning toward the unwelcome is a place of practice.

The best and most beautiful things in the world cannot be seen or even touched. They must be felt with the heart.

—HELEN KELLER

CHAPTER 4

You Are More Than Your Feelings

There's a song I love from the Broadway show *The Book of Mormon*. It's a cheeky parody number about culturally repressive ways of dealing with our feelings. The bit has a religious teacher counseling someone that when you start to have an "unacceptable" feeling, you should just "turn it off." It strikes me funny because it's true—it's in many ways what we have been conditioned to try to do. When I was growing up, it was communicated to me in subtle and not so subtle ways that only a certain range of feelings were allowed. The ones that were especially not allowed were sadness and anger—which was ironic, because there was actually so much sadness and so much anger in our house. Because there were only limited emotions we were able to express, I had to act like I wasn't sad and wasn't angry. I learned that I had to "turn it off, like a light switch." This made for a confusing existence; I felt so much rage and so much pain but had no place to express those feelings. They would inevitably come out in little bursts, and yet there was no way to express how I felt in any kind of healing way. Of course, the truth is that we can't just turn our feelings off. We need to find wiser ways to deal with them.

We have this cultural thing where people will look away and say "I'm thinking" to avoid being vulnerable. We throw that excuse over the wound of our tender hearts. In college, I was inspired by a friend to go back to therapy for the first time since I was a kid. This particular therapist's method was to maintain eye contact and stay connected in the midst of difficult feelings. I found it excruciating. So, of course, I started going three or four times a week for two-hour sessions! They were so painful, but I could see I needed to change my relationship to the feelings I was hiding. I found I had such a hard time feeling exposed, not knowing what I was going to say, and maintaining eye contact. I felt that these horribly embarrassing feelings would be revealed as I continued looking at this therapist. I would look away, and he would say, "Why are you looking away, and what are you looking away from?" I would say, "I'm thinking," because I didn't want to be so exposed emotionally. I was afraid. He was so courageous in his steadfastness in staying with whatever it was. He allowed me to finally explore the rage and sorrow that, for a long time, I hadn't even been able to admit that I had.

IN RELATIONSHIP

With the therapist's help I began to realize a new possibility. I understood another level of what Sensei White had said to me: "You will never be free until you can be still with your pain." With that therapist I learned a new and deep lesson: how to be still *in the exposure of relationship*. I learned how to be vulnerable and not move away, how to express these feelings that felt monstrous. Over time I learned that I had the same kind of depth of rage as I had grown up surrounded by and felt victimized by. I had told myself a story of being the *victim* of rage, as opposed to also being a person who has rage and sorrow and fear.

In a relationship, we can learn how to be still while becoming vulnerable. Recently, Chodo and I were heading out to lead a retreat. I was at the kitchen sink washing my breakfast bowl, and I turned around to see that Chodo was already dressed and ready to head out. The baby in me felt scared. *He is leaving me.* I looked into his eyes and said, "The story I am telling myself is you are leaving me." He looked at me and said, "That's just your crazy part." Then he walked over to me, held my shoulders, and kissed me. "I will see you in a few minutes. Enjoy your shower." At once the old irrational fear disappeared. It arose, I gave voice to it, and I have a relationship with my gorgeous husband who can hold my crazy and connect and I can hold his crazy and connect.

Over time we can practice going from being in our crazy scared place to being in loving relationship. It takes the mutual willingness to be vulnerable and to connect. If we find the right relationship to do that in, with someone who has done their own work, we can learn to be like the Buddha under the Bodhi tree. He learned how to stay steady while all the things that he feared came at him. He learned to stay in relationship with them. That way, relationships become, for us, like the Bodhi tree.

Feeling the Feelings

My therapist had a generous space to hold my deep feelings that surged like a volcano. How do we learn how to offer that both to ourselves and to others? That is the journey, but many times, in our suffering, we just want to go back to turning it off. You'll see people leaving communities or relationships or ghosting people because we don't know how to be soft in our bellies. We don't know how to be soft and stay with our feelings of rage and discomfort. We can learn! On the other hand, we can create space in relationship where we can be known and explore what it's like to have a full range of feelings and what it's like to allow feelings to flow through us without our being afraid of them.

We feel that we don't know who we would be if we allowed ourselves to feel whatever we're feeling, if we stopped trying to control the narrative. The reason we don't want certain feelings is because we over-identify with them. We think that having certain feelings makes us a certain kind of person: an angry one, a weak one, a bad one, a failure. We can create a prison for ourselves by locking ourselves in as the jailer and saying "That's how I am. That's who I am."

Ninety-Nine Curves

My college therapist was also modeling for me what I would ultimately have to learn to do for myself. Attentive, vulnerable relationship with another human being is a powerful context in which to embrace our feelings, and there are lots of times in life when that's not available. For some people it may never be. What are they to do? The Buddha, under the Bodhi tree, was alone. He had been abandoned by five companions who were all about turning off their feelings. They were hardcore ascetics who thought young Siddhartha had gone soft. The Buddha needed to face his fears with his own wisdom and compassion. If there is no one to hold us steady, we need to learn to hold ourselves steady like that, one shaky step at a time.

In the Zen tradition we sometimes work with koans, which are records of the dialogues or questions of ancient masters that we contemplate until we penetrate their meaning for ourselves (for more on that, see chapter 15). A favorite koan of mine is "How do you go straight on the path of ninety-nine curves?" In practice, we can begin to learn this through walking meditation. Practicing a slow version of kinhin, a Zen-style walking meditation, we take one half step, and then the next, feeling the heel, then the arch, and then the pads of your toes lifting off the ground, then coming down again, and then the other heel beginning to lift up and slowly putting the next one down. Working with feeling is equal to our willingness to be that slow and intentional, one half step at a time, so that we can go straight on the road with ninety-nine curves, one little step at a time. This is how we learn to feel the desire to turn it off, to stay in the discomfort, and to allow the feeling of not being liked or not being valued, for example, without flying from it into reactivity or internalizing it into self-hatred. I imagine people have been feeling this for 300,000 years as *Homo sapiens*, learning to go against the stream, going against our habit of the very human quality of aversion to our feelings and learning how to move in a different way. I think of little creatures padding their way out of the water and onto the land as they're born and move into the world. I feel this as I consider my own experience when learning to have that feeling and slowly making my way onto land with it.

Walking Meditation

Form a fist with your left hand and tuck your thumb into it. Wrap your right hand around your left fist. Place your hands on your solar plexus, the sensitive point just under the bottom ribs. Face the backs of your hands away from your body, and rest your wrists on your belly. Hold your forearms parallel to the ground or floor. Pull your elbows away from your body slightly.

Look downward at a forty-five-degree angle with a soft gaze. Put your right foot forward. Land on your heel. Let the ball of your foot touch the ground, then your toes. Repeat for the left foot. Be aware of the heel, ball, and toes touching the ground. Be aware of your breathing. Allow feelings to come up without judgment. Let them come and let them go. Be aware of the sensations of walking and the breath.

Going straight on the road of ninety-nine curves is a place of practice.

BABY MIND

Angulimala, a student of the Buddha, received his bizarre name (it means "finger garland") in a gruesome way. Angulimala, the story goes, was a serious practitioner of an ancient type of yoga. He was close with his teacher, and his fellow students were jealous. They decided they would remove him as the teacher's pet by tricking him and creating distance between him and their teacher. Angulimala's fellow students told him that what the teacher wanted from him was for him to make a garland of 108 fingers, like you see on the goddess Kali. They told him that in order to prove his devotion to the teacher, he would have to kill 108 people and take their fingers. Angulimala was horrified, but he said he would do it.

Many of us have been set up in ways like this—if usually less gruesome ones—in a million little ways by our society. We are told we need to marry this kind of person, or we need to have this kind of job, or we need to ignore the promptings of our conscience, and we turn our face away from the cost to ourselves and others—we can't do what our hearts say to do, we have to do what we're told to do. How did the perpetrators in my life become like that? How does it happen to us when we are the perpetrators? No baby I've ever met wants to intentionally cause harm to other people. Angulimala didn't want to do that either, but because he was afraid of losing something he loved, he lost touch with his inner feelings and core values. The society he moved in told him something was required that on his own he would never feel okay with, and he went along.

Finding Our People

Growing up, I didn't have a consistent person from whom I could get a reality check, which made me feel kind of crazy. I didn't know how to express what I thought was going on, and when I would say inside of my family what I thought was happening, people would often respond with "That isn't what is happening."

Like me, Angulimala didn't have the right people to check in with. His fellow students were so caught in their jealousy that they couldn't help. All of us need someone reliable to check with, people who are reliable witnesses. When we don't have that our individual worlds can become frightening. Angulimala had lost touch with his own inner compass; he did not have his own sense of "that's not okay." It's so destabilizing to have no sense inside of ourselves of what's okay and what's not okay. He was in a position in his life where he wasn't able to simply say, "That's totally not happening. I'm not doing that." Who knows what had happened to Anguli-mala in his life that he had learned he didn't have that space in his life, a steady connection to his own values that was stronger than his reactive feelings.

This can and does happen in power relationships. In Anguli-mala's relationship to his teacher, the sense of what constituted his path became completely centered in his teacher, not in himself. I've seen this again and again in spiritual communities, where a leader who wants to be in control comes into contact with wounded students. That disempowers people's own sense of agency and their connection to their own feelings; in other words, it blocks the development of the path to freedom. We need to learn how to find that ground in ourselves, in healthy relationships. How do we find the people who can be a refuge for us where we can work it out?

Dirty Potato Practice

Korean Zen master Seung Sahn said that a good community is like dirty potatoes in a barrel—we rub up against one another to get clean. That barrel is where we learn to be with our feelings without becoming them. If a community is working, we're going to feel the full range of feelings in it. If it's okay enough, if it's good enough, then we can learn how to stay. Then we can learn something; we can stop overidentifying with our feelings and actually change. Bear in mind that no one is going to be perfect. I often tell my students, "I will disappoint you!" And then I like to say, "And I'm committed to being with you in the disappointment." This makes for a good beginning. We need to find a "good enough" teacher. We need to find a good enough community, which is one where you can be dirty potatoes in a barrel.

Checking In

How many movie and TV plots where it all goes wrong center around people not checking in? Things are misunderstood, stories are cemented, actions are taken, and the whole thing begins in a misunderstanding: a belief that was never investigated. Avoiding this comes down to asking ourselves, "What is the story I'm telling myself right now?" and checking carefully what the basis for it is in reality. Imagine if Angulimala had someone he could check in with, and he had done that. How much trouble do we get in because we don't check things out with the people around us? Of course, Angulimala couldn't do that because his companions in the spiritual life were just as compromised by their own wounds as he was, but he could have checked in with the person he was afraid to ask—his teacher. He also could have sought out someone outside his community. He could have gone outside his comfort zone to seek out a reality check. Perhaps.

Angulimala didn't do that, though. He started doing the horrible task, becoming this person called Finger Garland. He was known as a killer, and people throughout the rural villages of India became terrified of him. Finally, he obtained 107 fingers; he was almost done. He could present this mala to the teacher he thought wanted it.

The Buddha had heard about Angulimala and his gruesome task and went into the woods to find him. He found his student there, so filled with rage and so wanting to finish this already. The Buddha knew Angulimala would come after him in order to collect that last finger, so once the Buddha found him, he turned around and began walking away. Angulimala started chasing the Buddha, but no matter how fast Angulimala ran, he couldn't catch him, even though the Buddha appeared to be walking slowly ahead of him. Finally, Angulimala shouted at the Buddha: "Stop!"

The Buddha turned around and simply said, "Angulimala, I stopped long ago. How about you?"

Something about that stunning reply awakened Angulimala out of this terrible dream. He became a student of the Buddha. By the way, what the Buddha did when he said "I've stopped, how about you?" also teaches a lesson on the side about how a good teacher teaches. A good teacher will always be pointing back to the student and saying "I've done that, how about you? How are you going to do that?" Not "Do that like I did."

Angulimala had been overcome by his fear of losing his connection to his teacher. He did not know how to work with his feelings or how to greet them with the needed mix of acceptance and skepticism. If we try to push a feeling down, it becomes more powerful, yet if we enact the feeling like Angulimala did, it becomes an incredible weight. If we hold back a feeling too long, it becomes like a wild horse and takes us away. It's learning how to stay *stopped* like the Buddha, how to stop that whole game, that changes things. How do we learn how to stop?

Stopping

One of my favorite ways to stop is to stand and meditate in a grocery store line. Let's practice this form of stopping together.

Find somewhere to rest comfortably inside yourself. Let your body settle in a way that feels good. Make whatever microadjustments are needed. Be aware of your breathing, and then let your awareness of your breath draw you into your lower belly. Allow your belly to be soft. Let your awareness arrive fully in the body, flowing throughout it until you can feel the sensations throughout your body. When feelings arise, let them come and go without picking them up. As Japanese Zen teacher Kosho Uchiyama liked to say, "Open the hand of thought." No matter what arises, let it go. Pay particular attention to the feelings, thoughts, and opinions of whatever arises, and see if you can gently welcome and allow it without reacting. Let the feeling arise, increase in intensity, and fade away again. This is "stopping."

Watching the river of thoughts and feelings from the riverbank is a place of practice.

RESPONSIBILITY

We have the capacity to stop being run by our feelings and by what we think we should feel or shouldn't feel. Angulimala *was* his feelings. He was a devoted student who would do anything for his teacher, so when he was asked to do something unconscionable, he couldn't stand against it. He was driven by his fear and his desire. The truth is, he couldn't feel his deeper feelings, the feelings of his heart, which were buried under all the reactive feelings he was identified with.

Can we see ourselves in this? Can we be the Buddha to ourselves, to our inner Angulimala? It was only through feeling my feelings totally that I began to realize they were just what was coming through, and that I could let them pass by. It was my trying to control them that allowed them to control me. We cannot run from our feelings, so we might as well learn how to allow them and take responsibility for them. When we stop being run by toxic feelings, the deeper feelings of the heart show themselves, and a new life can begin, moment by moment.

After Angulimala became a monk his troubles were not over. That's not the way the whole catastrophe works, is it? He might have thought, *Well, I stopped. I gave up killing and again became a student of the Buddha, got my head straightened out. That shit trip is over.* Not so fast, Angie.

People in the nearby villages remembered what Angulimala had done. When he would go walking through villages on the traditional alms rounds of a Buddhist monk, they would shout at him and call him names. Worse, they would throw stones at him. It's understandable, isn't it? He had killed 107 people. He would come back to see the Buddha, all bloody and beat up, and ask him what to do.

"Bear it, Angulimala, bear it," the Buddha would tell him. The Buddha told Angulimala that what he was going through was part of the process of transformation. When we accept our feelings and take responsibility for them, that's not the end of it. We have to deal with the messes that we've made, if we've made any (and probably we have). We have to bear the working out of those feelings in our bodies, which can take some time. If we mistakenly think, after we've felt our feelings, that they're now going to go away forever, along with the traces they've left in our lives and relationships, then the next time they arise we may start the whole cycle of avoidance and/or enactment again.

Pema Chodron points out that if we don't process feelings and take responsibility for them, what we tend to do instead is gather our armies. We find others who agree with us and who amplify the feelings of righteousness that we're hiding our pain behind. All you have to do is scan the newspaper to see how the world is filled with people finding and amassing armies of others who agree with them. The other group then becomes the hated group. The revolutionary move is to take the backward step and turn the light within to where it hasn't reached yet. It is learning how to realize, moment by moment, that we're not just our feelings. We do that by allowing them their own life without being possessed by them.

PROJECTION

In my childhood home I was taught to hate Germans and Poles for what they had done to our people. The first German I met was named Elka. She was an exchange student at my high school, and she was so sweet. Meeting her was part of what got me thinking I'd like to go on one of Bernie Glassman's Bearing Witness retreats at

Auschwitz. On those retreats, you would sit on the tracks on which the victims arrived in cattle cars and recite the names of the murdered for the whole day. I realized, while doing that, that I had all that in me: the killers, the killed. It's easy to say who's right and who's wrong, but it's harder to be with the killer in you, your inner Angulimala, and to understand that we kill with our feelings, thoughts, and actions too. We are responsible for how we continue to deal with our unprocessed feelings, and for whether we continue the cycle of trauma and abuse or not. How do we do that? We can just be there, feeling what we're feeling, allowing the feelings to both arise and cease without controlling them. We can learn to feel them as they are in the body, wherever they are, and breathe into them. This is how we can stay engaged in the nature of reality. If we try to evade feelings that hurt or that we are ashamed of, liking some feelings, not liking others, identifying and dis-identifying and ping-ponging around, then we'll have a ping-pong life. When we accept that a feeling is present, know that we are more than that feeling, and take responsibility for it, then we can move into something new. Feeling the feelings without becoming the feelings has become a place of deep practice.

Our natural attitude is to feel lucky when things are going our way, but when we get on the path, our sense of what is really lucky, what is really fortunate, can shift. Bhadra, one of the first Buddhist nuns, wrote a poem about this over two thousand years ago:

You always considered yourself lucky
because things seemed to work out
the way you wanted.

Now luck has a different meaning.

Lucky to be walking a Path
that finds
peace
in the arising
and passing away of each
present
moment.

Regardless
of how things work out—
or don't.

My friend Ira Byock talks about imagining people well, imagining ourselves well, imagining a different response. There's a story that's evocative of this. A tenzo (monastery cook) is overseeing the preparation of a meal. As it is about to be served, he realizes he forgot the soup. The tenzo gets a bunch of vegetables and makes a quick soup super fast—maybe too fast! Still, it is served impeccably. The head monk picks up the spoon. On the spoon is a snake's head. He calls the tenzo over, and the tenzo bows, takes the snake's head off the spoon, pops it in his mouth, eats it, and leaves. It's done.

Here, the tenzo moves from shame into a healthy embarrassment—*I did that*, his action says. He's able to do that because he's not afraid of his feelings, and he's not trying to control the narrative. That's eating the snake's head. When we do that instead of reinforcing an old identity, we can do something new. As Thich Nhat Hanh said, "We have more possibilities available in each moment than we realize."

DEWDROP

While on call one night, I was paged at three in the morning. At the hospital, someone was actively dying, and the family wanted me to come. I arrived around four a.m., stepping into the cacophony of the emergency room. It was a Friday night, usually a busy night in the ER, and I asked where this family was. Behind a curtain, there was this slight, small fern of a man curled up in the bed. His well-dressed family was standing with their backs pressed against the curtain, as far away from him as possible. The feeling of fear was tangible.

This was early in my clinical training, and I remember thinking, *Oh god, what am I going to do?* Then I realized—that wasn't my feeling. I got interested in that feeling of *I don't know what to do*, and I realized that I had taken on that feeling the moment I walked in. We walk into rooms all the time and experience them as sad or energetic rooms. That was a fearful, bewildered room, so I took on that feeling: *I don't know what to do, I'm scared, I feel helpless.* Instead of continuing to take it on, I got curious. I felt tight in my chest, and then I looked at the family pressed up against the curtain. Their breath was all in their chests; their eyes were wide. I said, "What's happening?"

They said, "We don't know what to do. We don't know what's happening."

I saw, when I looked over at the father on the bed, that he was clearly mouthing something. I said, "Do you know what he's saying?"

They said, "No."

So I went over, and he was whispering. This little man was whispering, "Hold me, hold me, hold me."

I gently touched his hand and I said, "I'll be right back, hold on."

I told them, "He wants to be held."

They said, "We can't do that."

I said, "If you hold me, I'll hold him." I don't know what came over me. If we don't stay with the fear feeling, and we explore the feeling instead, things can shift. I wanted to help them get close, so I said, "One of you keep your hand on me, and the rest hold each other, and we'll make a little chain."

I gently leaned across the bed and held the man around his shoulders, my arm on his arm. He said, "Ahhhhhh. More, more, more."

I ended up crawling into the bed with him, holding him, as his wife was touching me on my shoulder, and I was holding him, embracing him, this man. And he said, "Ahhhhhh, thank you, thank you." And he died.

I continued to hold him for some time, and his body began to cool as it does as we lose our life energy. This incredible tenderness came into the room. The family circled around the bed close, and they said, "We've never hugged." It reminded me of how often we hold back our feelings. We don't know this family's story, but we do know that they didn't know how to hold one another, and in the end it's what the father wanted the most. It's what, in some way, allowed him to die while feeling held.

Sometimes we get so caught in our fear that we forget to take risks. Emotionally, we tend to hold back our depth of feeling. We forget to put our ear to someone's lips. We forget to be curious about how another person is feeling, about what we're feeling, not as something to resist or act out on, but as something to hold with compassion and be curious about. That's how we allow more tenderness and new possibilities, so when we're not caught by the feeling we can actually be there. How can you practice widening out so that you can feel your feelings and expand? How are you more than your feelings? How do you reflect on this? When we engage new possibilities and new actions, things can change. Something new can happen, like the dewdrops we find on the thousands of tips of grass in the morning.

The happiness of your life depends upon the quality of your thoughts: therefore, guard accordingly, and take care that you entertain no notions unsuitable to virtue and reasonable nature.

—MARCUS AURELIUS

CHAPTER 5

You Are Not Just Your Thoughts

There is an awesome quote that floats around on the swirls and eddies of the internet—no one really knows who said it, and it has been ascribed to everybody from the Buddha to Jimi Hendrix: "Watch your feelings, as they become your thoughts, your thoughts become your words, your words become your actions, your actions become your character."

Here is where we find the importance of what we were exploring in the last chapter—responsibility. This river of continuity is important to explore so that we can untangle our tangles. I grew up in a family, like many families, where feelings would arise, and then the thoughts about those feelings became words, which in turn became the actions and the character—the culture—of our family. It all came pouring into the dysfunctional container of our family like a polluted stream, feelings around fear, insecurity, abandonment, vulnerability, and sadness—to name a few. There was not enough self-awareness of or wise relationship to these feelings, and as a result, the people I knew were in fact often more like fire hoses. They were either on or off, and when the hose was on, it could knock you off your seat.

REDIRECTING THE STREAM

Take a moment to pause. In the following section, I am sharing my experience of contemplating self-harm. If you or someone you love is struggling in this way, help is available. There are resources available for you at the end of the book.

One night during my high school years, my feeling of being trapped and overwhelmed became so severe that I became suicidal. I was actually sitting with a razor blade in the bathroom looking down at my wrists. This was in the midst of the time I was being bullied a lot, and there was so much fear in the house too, piling onto the suffocation I felt. It felt like there was nowhere to go. This was just before I met Sensei White. I felt very alone and had no idea where I could find refuge. My thoughts all said one thing: I had to get out.

What led me to the bathroom that evening was yet another scary incident in my house. I would often go into the bathroom, because it was one of the few doors with a lock. I didn't know what to do with my fear, so it fed me thoughts insisting that the only way out was to kill myself. I felt invaded and terrorized both at school and at home. Yet it was my thoughts that had cornered me. It's the thoughts that actually became the prison; the feelings were just fear. The thoughts were where I had leverage, though I couldn't see it yet. I needed to understand that between feeling and thought was a space of freedom.

I can still remember the feeling of the top of my hand on the cold bathroom counter. I remember looking at the veins in my left wrist and holding a razor blade in my right hand. I was thinking, *I have to get out, I have to get out.* I took the razor and grazed it across my wrist to see what it felt like. Then, this new thought came out, like lightning flashing in the sky: *Is it really true that this is the only way?* I don't know where that thought came from, but it shocked me out of what I was thinking of doing.

An immediate response came from inside: *There* has *to be another way.* That was a pivotal moment for me, when I started turning toward the wheel of practice, although I didn't know it yet. I walked over to the window and looked out into the backyard. Outside the window was a crescent of beautiful giant pine trees; above their tips, I saw, was the sky. The sun had just set, and the sky was a deep and vivid blue. Suddenly the moment turned deeply magical, just as the sky subtly deepened into black.

Somehow, then and there, I found the courage to become the sky. It seems like a funny thing to say, but that's what it felt like. I saw that the sky just keeps changing—bright blue, gray, purple, black—and I remember thinking that I too could change. I too had depths beyond the clouds, beyond light and dark. At the same time, in a way that might seem odd, our two cats appeared in my mind. We had a cat named Bruce and another named Sneakers. Bruce was female, actually, but it was my turn to name the cat, and I loved the name Bruce (perhaps it was because there was a boy at school that I had a major crush on named Bruce). Bruce and Sneakers would fight terribly. They would go at each other so badly they would tear huge chunks out of each other's fur and flesh. The thing was, you just had to separate Bruce and Sneakers, and then they were fine. I had to figure out a way, like Sneakers and Bruce, to create separation in my own mind.

When I went to the window, open to another way, everything I saw—the trees, the sky, suddenly seemed courageous. In seeing that, I thought, *You can be with change, you can adapt, you can find a new way.* A new way for reality to turn. It was the thought that provided a doorway to walk through. The pine trees and the sky, the space between Bruce and Sneakers, the thought that I could survive, all came together in this creative mash-up from the DJ of my mind. It was saying, "There are other possibilities here, other ways to think." That's what inspired me, a few days later, to take my bicycle and go to the strip mall and find the karate school.

I saw at that moment, with the help of the sky, that I didn't need to be cornered. I had felt frightened and desperate, and I saw that it was actually my thoughts that were blinding me. That's not to say that conditions were not terrifying and painful, fearful and real, yet there was something else: this light, a door, a window to new roads. I needed to find a different space. Discipline, at first in the form of karate, would end up being a path for me, but what I needed to find first was a different physical space, like the cats, who had different food, litter trays, and house areas. I found my own space at the dojo.

When we're caught in a cycle of thoughts, we think that our thoughts are true. This is what led me to a razor's edge, thinking it was the only option. When you realize that there must be another way than these entrapping thoughts, and you are open to the possibility that these thoughts are not true, then at that moment you are more than your thoughts. The thoughts have a vote, but they're not calling the shots anymore. When you do that, you can hear something new, as I did.

Take a moment to pause. Put your palm on your lower belly, two inches below your belly button. Feel the breath move your hand. What happens to your mind?

Allowing change is a place of practice.

THE DHARMA OF FORMS AND SOUNDS

As a kid (and, honestly, still as an adult), I was obsessed with Greek myths. All the great hero stories I loved so much show us that although there is always trouble, it is how people work with the trouble that makes them who they are. The protagonist would get help from all kinds of unlikely places. Chiron helped Hercules, Jason, and Achilles. Hermes and Athena helped Perseus with his tangle with Medusa. For me, the pine trees and the sky were the mysterious helpers.

The thirteenth-century Zen master Dogen wrote about "the Dharma of sounds and forms," which is what I heard that night. *Dharma* refers to a truth that sets us free. Dogen said that the whole world is teaching Dharma all the time, and we can hear it if we pay attention. When you are receptive to being more than your thoughts, something new can happen. You can hear what the world is preaching to you about life all the time. You realize you can think in a new way and imagine new possibilities of action.

In that moment I saw I still had the capacity to be receptive. That meant possibility. That is wisdom, knowing that there are other possibilities, not just how I am thinking about a situation at the moment. The receptivity to the world beyond my thought— light, color, sensation—opened me up to mysterious help. When you realize that the story you're telling yourself is not necessarily the gospel truth, then you can tell yourself another story. We can ask ourselves, *What story am I telling myself?* This can lead us out of the struggle and the tangle of our thoughts. This is what I learned in the inglorious setting of the baby-blue-tiled bathroom, my mind full of thoughts telling me that there was no solution.

Beyond Positive/Negative

Like our feelings, our thoughts become a problem when instead of taking care of them, we just don't want to deal with them. We intuit, inside ourselves, that it's our thoughts that are making us suffer. Many people come to a spiritual path because we want to escape our thoughts. "Drop your story," we're told, but sometimes it's not so simple—we have a lot of stories! We'll do anything to substitute good thoughts for bad ones that are judgy, angry, obsessive, or negative. If we can do that, it will be bliss 24-7, we think. We want to *be* how other people *look* on social media.

The basic approach to thoughts is to welcome everything, to push away nothing. We tend to divide thoughts into positive and negative, which can be a helpful pointer and yet can easily be misused. We can begin to fear the "negative" thoughts, to react to them with tension and shame. I find a better approach is to ask, "What is life giving for me?" We can let go of the thoughts that are not life giving, but there is no reason to be afraid of them. Tension, aversion, fear, shame, and other emotions wrap up our attention in the thought and give it a different kind of toxic life. If we can relate to our thoughts without pushing them away, pretending they aren't there, or being ashamed of them, then they can take on their true dimensions in our mind, which is, of course, nothing. They are just passing thoughts, the same kind of psychic effluvium that every other human being is dealing with.

The Spiritual Bypass

Many people come to spiritual and meditation practices to perform the bait and switch called the spiritual bypass. We want to not think the way we think, and so instead of improving the way we relate to our minds, we apply a spiritual coating and pretend we don't think that way. We tell ourselves—and perform for others—that we are 100 percent mindfulness, empathy, focus, or whatever the current trend is. *I'm just going to do that; that's how I'll be from now on, starting this moment,* we think. It's like we cover ourselves with sticky notes: *I'm happy, I'm mindful.* Yet what we really need is to notice our habitual thoughts and stories, as painful as this can be. As Carl Jung wrote, "One does not become enlightened by imagining figures of light, but by making the darkness conscious."

We don't know how to deal with our painful feelings or our suffering, and we don't know the problem is actually our thoughts. Often when we come to spiritual practice this way, we bounce around from one spiritual trip to another. That was me to a T when I was younger—I had no idea how to work with my thoughts, and I was so invested in my stories—they were my identity. I was the victim, the bullied kid, the trapped one. I was so afraid I would get hurt if I let anyone close, so when I would go into a community, it would not be too long before those stories would come into my mind: *This is not a safe place. I'm disappointed. I'm going to get hurt here. My needs aren't going to be met.* I was with many different teachers and communities, but I was trailing around with the thoughts and painful stories about me and my self-worth in my big black bag.

It was not until after I saw my pattern and settled down in a community that I realized what I'd been doing. After many years of this, I already knew I was a lone wolf, wounded and avoiding the pack. I knew a lot, and that was part of the problem! I knew so much about what I was afraid of and what I couldn't do. I had fallen again into believing there couldn't be another story, and my thoughts were shackling me.

Shattering the Ridge Pole

Shakyamuni Buddha, when he was looking for a way out of suffering, tried a lot of different things. In the end, they all came down either to ways to flee from reality or to conquer it by force of will. At a certain point, though, he thought, *Enough. I've got to sit down and face myself, face things as they are, just as they are.* He vowed not to get up from under the Bodhi tree until he had found a solution. At a certain point that's what we have to do. We have to put our stake in the ground and say, "I am here, and I can't keep running, and I can't keep pretending I can will my life to be the way I want it." Like Angulimala, we need to stop. If we don't do that, we'll keep bypassing. Some people have the opposite pattern from that of the lone wolf: They will use a certain spiritual community as a hideout where they can stay for a long time—maybe their whole lives—and the whole time manage not to address the thought patterns that tangle up their lives and the lives of their loved ones. That's their own flavor of bypassing. There are so many ways. You can be immersed in a yogic path, a pillar of an organization, but you still haven't taken responsibility and turned toward your stories and said, "Are these really true?" And so maybe you are even comfortable to an extent, but you're not free.

When the Buddha completely broke through all of the thoughts with which he was entrapping himself, he said, "No more will I build a house of sorrow. The ridge pole is shattered." He saw that his thoughts, how he was working with his mind, were what kept him enslaved. Knowing he was not just his thoughts, he could come back to his body, the body of the universe. "I and all beings attain the Way together," he said, because as he felt his tangles falling away, the world was newborn in front of him.

REFUGE IN THE BODY

When the Buddha came back to himself, he came back to his body and the body of the world. He was part of the universe, and he was no longer separated—the teaching we can hear when we open up beyond our tangles and learn from the world, which is so much bigger than our thoughts about it.

Shundo Aoyama Roshi, a contemporary Zen Buddhist nun, in her book *Zen Seeds*, quotes a poem written by a Japanese schoolboy that goes:

In the middle of Japan, surrounded by
The Pacific Ocean, the Sea of Okhotsk,
The Japan Sea, and the East China Sea,
At Furokawa First Elementary School,
Right now I am fighting.

Sometimes when I need perspective, I consider the Cosmic Snake, a visible galaxy they found with the Hubble Space Telescope. It's a galaxy distant from us, peppered with regions of star formation. It looks like a long snake, at least through our telescopes. It's a moment where I realize, "Oh! That also exists." The rings of Saturn exist. Pygmy nuthatches exist. In fact, a zillion wonderful and strange things exist alongside all of the thoughts we have, and 99.9 percent of them proceed on their majestic way, seemingly with nary a thought in our direction. What reality actually is, who knows?

For me, this connected recently when I witnessed a customer at a grocery store treating a cashier poorly. My first thought was *What a terrible person.* I was so sure I was right; it was obvious. I told myself a story about how this customer was being so abusive. That's how quick and efficient my absolute power of judgment is. I knew that this person was bad and that the cashier was wonderful. Yet, remembering the Cosmic Snake, I thought, *What do we know about anything?* When it was my turn to check out, I asked the cashier, "What happened?" She said, "Oh, that was my boyfriend. I did a terrible thing to him. I hurt him so much, and he's so hurt and angry, and I understand. I don't know if he'll forgive me." We looked at each other, and she had tears in her eyes. Much like my experience of fear that Chodo was leaving me, the whole story I was telling was not true. When we are so sure, we can get into such trouble.

Working through Fear

Because of my history, the feeling of fear is still a powerful place of practice for me. The fear doesn't go away, but how I work with it now continues to change. Thoughts like *I'm in trouble, I'm in danger—mortal danger!* can come to me quickly. When that happens, I ground myself in my body and in my breath. I come back from that by coming into the softness of the belly, coming into my breath, placing my hands on my belly, putting my feet on the ground, and remembering *I'm here, here, here.* I experience the widening out like I did in that bathroom in my childhood home, looking out. I also ask myself, *Is that true that I am in literal danger? Am I safe right now?* My thoughts may say, *Yes, yes, you are in grave danger!* But am I really? Unless I'm about to be mugged or hit by a hurricane, I can realize that I am often not in literal danger. There is nothing that is really about to hurt me or threaten me at the level I am feeling afraid. I am safe. I reach down to touch the earth like the Buddha. We can do that any time. Right now, we can take the earth as our witness.

Coming into Consciousness

We set the Dharma wheel in motion to leave the house of sorrow. *Ichi-go ichi-e.* One moment, one chance. In each moment we have this opportunity of working with our thoughts instead of being defined by them. On the other hand, if we just go unconscious— well, we all know what happens. We start to build a character that is unconscious. When we're unconscious, we can build a life based entirely on appearances or around believing a whole house of cards built of thoughts that may not be true. Once we know that we are more than just our bodies, feelings, and thoughts, then we can cultivate the path, and the path is the steady cultivation of conditions that allow us to leave the house of sorrow. The door out of the house of sorrow is a question, or what our friend Hongzhi Zhengjue called "inquiry." How do you cultivate a tender inquiry into your daily experience?

DAFFODILS

Our thoughts become our character, and I've heard so many painful and limiting thoughts. "That's too hard for me, too scary." That's a popular one. We say these sentences, we feed them with our attention, and then we become a person who finds things too hard and too scary. But is it really true? What else is true?

I know a woman in her seventies who had developed this idea that she couldn't grow any further. She had retired. Her cat died. She didn't get out much. She was withdrawing into herself, and she felt very alone. We began to have these conversations, and she would keep saying, "I can't do it. It's too hard. I can't get out. The way is shut."

I asked her, "Is that really true? Is that your actual experience?"

She said, "Yes, it is."

"How do you know?" I asked, to open up a little space.

This surprised her. She said, "Maybe I don't know."

I said, "Have you gone outside, just to take a little peek?"

Slowly she took a peek and began to see. "My goodness, it's spring outside. Daffodils!" I asked her, what were they like? "They're so beautiful, so cute, so perky," she told me, "and guess what—the tulips are coming!" Slowly she began to do more. "Is it true?" I asked her. "Was it too hard to see the daffodils?"

"No," she said, "of course it wasn't hard to see the daffodils." Then she came to see me, all the way downtown. After a couple of weeks of fretting about how, she up and got on the subway. Here was this beautiful person, beautiful like we all are, but so trapped in distorted, painful ideas that felt like such a big deal. They're just flickers of electricity in the brain, but we can let them rule our lives.

The truth is, asking whether our thoughts are really true may start out scary, but it can get fun. It starts with stories about how we feel, about what we can do, about what others think, but it can go deeper and deeper. Where is the point where we end and the universe begins? Is it really true that we end at our skin? Is it really true that I know who or what I am? Is it really true that there is something to defend?

When we change our thoughts, our feelings get less scary. We can choose new words and new actions, and that means our character can change too. We are not in charge of how quickly our thoughts change—sometimes it's fast, and sometimes it's slow—but we are responsible for questioning them. That's how things begin to shift, and the opportunity to pivot arrives.

The mouth of the wolf is not the end of the world.

—JAMES LAPINE

CHAPTER 6

Confronting the Giants and Their
Wheels of Suffering

When we are confronting the three giants, we are in the liberating land of the second noble truth. I know what you're probably wondering right now: *What was the first noble truth again?* Well, there are actually four, and we'll get there. What the four truths are and what makes them noble will become clear as we go.

The first noble truth is that there is suffering. That's what we've been exploring so far, and it's something we need to acknowledge before we can look at the three others. The path begins with admitting that we are suffering.

The second noble truth is that suffering has a cause. The cause of suffering is thirst (the literal meaning of "tanha," sometimes translated as desire or craving), the sense of lack, obsessive desire, deficiency, and addictive propulsion that causes us to cling to things as if that clinging would make us happy. If you take a moment to reflect on this, you can see the reality of this in your own experience. To cling to things is to be unwilling for them to change or to be other than we wish them to be. We want them to be more (or less) than they are; we want them to stay when they are in the process of going or to arrive before they do. All of these efforts are shot through with delusion about the way things and people actually behave, and greed and anger come in their wake. Thus, this clinging takes the shape of greed, anger, and delusion. What hurts is not that things change; what hurts is that we're holding on to them *while* they change.

We need to understand these three elemental forces of greed, anger, and delusion and how they wreak havoc in our lives as we set off on the Eightfold Path. But first, what is the nobility of the Four Noble Truths? Why do we call them noble? We've been exploring the different levels of suffering and how we're tangled up in it. There's nobility in that honesty and sobriety. Once we see that yes, I struggle, yes, I suffer, yes, I have meshugas, then we can look at the patterns that cause us to get so tangled up.

When people are acting out, there is no nobility in that. The nobility is in taking responsibility for our struggle. When we do that, the fact that we are fucked-up becomes nobility. The tangle and suffering can be used for a nobility of purpose. The change comes when we say, "Yeah I'm doing that; this is how I'm functioning, and I'm making myself and other people miserable." Then there are possibilities, and not until then.

This means facing giants.

GIANTS

Giants exist in every culture, from Greek to Norse, Hindu, Bulgarian, and Basque myths; they're even in the Bible. They disrupt our culture, our being, our social order. The nature of these three forces—greed, anger, and delusion—is that they are so powerful that they frighten us; they are forces in the world that we feel threatened by. What's also important about them is that they embody what is ancient—rooted in biology that even extends beyond our *Homo sapiens* line. Yet oftentimes we can get caught in thinking *It's* my *fear. It's* my *(fill in the blank).* The reality is that they are ancient and primordial forces, not personal. Greed, anger, and delusion have been around since the beginning of human time. In that way they are giants; they have existed throughout time.

It's helpful to realize that these giants are not human; they're simply energies that exist through life itself. If you watch our cat Bodhidharma Burrito, he gets scared, he wants things, he's confused—it's all the same. We beat ourselves up for having these energies and feelings that literally every living being has. That's a delusion. It's not our fault that we have these energies, but it is up to us to take responsibility for how they impact us and for our impact when they take us over.

The Absolute Bagel

I was in a bagel shop called Absolute Bagels, a wonderful place that people from all over New York City visit. It's run by a group of Buddhists from Thailand. A guy came in who was really tall and muscular, and kind of unhinged and probably struggling with some kind of mental illness. He was yelling, "Who is going to give me a bagel?" Everyone in the shop looked rather afraid, but the person behind the counter leaned over and said, "Hello, sir. I will make you a bagel." He said so gently, "How would you like your bagel?"

The man barked, "Cream cheese and tomato on a poppy seed bagel," and the worker made the bagel, wrapped it up nicely, and handed it to him.

The guy said, "This is cold, what the hell is wrong with you? Breakfast is supposed to be hot."

Everyone around was like *ugh, how ungrateful, how unkind*, and my friend behind the counter said, "Oh, I'm so sorry. You'd like it toasted."

The man said, "Yes, I'd like it toasted! Of course it's supposed to be toasted." So my friend remade it and gave it to him. The man ripped the paper the bagel came in open, shoved the food in his mouth, and yelled, "This is delicious!" Suddenly his energy shifted. He swallowed and enjoyed, his body relaxed a little bit, and he said, "I'm sorry that I was so rude. I was just so hungry."

The man behind the counter looked at him, smiled, and said, "I hope you enjoy the rest of your bagel," and the bagel-loving man left.

Our anger, which is like a little snowball, can become an avalanche, which is what happened with this man and happens with all of us. It is so important to slow down and to learn how to address anger in a new way. Meeting fire with fire is usually not skillful. In this case it was my friend's kindness in not taking things personally that turned the event around. It was through the medicine of generosity that he was able to tend to this giant.

HEALTHY EMBARRASSMENT

One way to address anger is to realize we have that giant in ourselves. Then we can recognize it in others and say, *Oh yeah, you too? We're in this together.* That's where compassion is. If we are not afraid of the giant that is coursing through us, that's the noble stance within the struggle and tangle. We need to realize that the giants are not personal. When we see the giants in ourselves, we can be paralyzed by shame and fear, which is not helpful. What's needed is something else, which I call healthy embarrassment. This is not embarrassment that the giants exist within us, but at the fact that we have cooperated with them. We have let them course through our lives or simply said, "That's who I am."

Years ago, while I was in college, I decided to go on a semester-long trip traveling across the country with the American historian Douglas Brinkley, studying the Beat poets and American history for three months on the road. I was so excited and intoxicated, but I didn't consider the impact my plans might have on my then lover, Tony, at all.

I was caught by the giant of greed. Not that I shouldn't have been excited about something wonderful and fabulous, but I didn't consider how Tony would feel—completely abandoned. They were so enraged about what an asshole I was, mostly because I hadn't checked in with them. It's not that they wouldn't have been happy for me; it was that I didn't even consider them. I was so ashamed because I thought of myself as someone who didn't act that way. My identity was that of a very caring person. It was right for me to confront the fact that I had acted badly, yet the paralyzing sense of shame that came over me was not helpful.

The reason that kind of shame is not helpful is that it gets in the way of positive action and keeps the focus on ourselves. The shame spiral, in that case, went like this for me: We got in a huge fight and both felt disconnected and pissed. Then, I felt terrible for causing harm. My image of myself as a loving, caring person crumbled. So, I worked extra hard writing cards, offering star lilies, and leaving desperate loving voice messages, all to try to reinstate my crumbled "nice person" self. This left me feeling like a victim, desperately trying to build back my Humpty Dumpty self. It didn't repair the relationship.

What I've been working with since that time is learning the joy of a healthy embarrassment as opposed to a toxic shame. It's good to be embarrassed when we do things that betray our own ethics and values because we are possessed by these giants. That's what they do—they compel us when we are possessed by these energies. Then our values go out the window.

The Buddha spoke of healthy embarrassment when he discussed what he called "the two bright qualities that protect the world." These are hiri (moral shame) and ottappa (fear of consequences). The first, hiri, is what I'm talking about. As described by the scholar-monk Bhikkhu Bodhi, it is rooted in self-respect. This is not the type of shame that causes suffering, deception, or self-loathing, but is the shame or embarrassment that someone with dignity or self-respect feels when they think about cooperating with a giant or realize that they have been in thrall to one.

We need to get curious about this feeling of embarrassment instead of being afraid of it. These giants are just doing what they do. Greed, anger, and delusion are just being themselves. When we think we're not supposed to feel them, it means we're not supposed to be in the world. This work is about being in the world, which means giants and witches and unicorns and the abyss are all part of it. We live in a world with giants, and they will be around much longer than we will. That's all true, yet we do have a choice about how we will relate to these energies. When they possess us, a healthy sense of embarrassment can help us take responsibility and recalibrate.

Reflection

Take a moment to ask yourself, "How can this embarrassment be good news? How can it be essential?"

Is there something you've been running from that might be better to embrace with a sense of healthy embarrassment? Can you allow yourself to be an imperfect human and do that and then move on, ready to try to meet the giant differently next time?

Moving from shame to healthy embarrassment is a place of practice.

PRINCE FIVE WEAPONS AND THE GIANT STICKY HAIR

Jataka tales are Indian folk tales about the Buddha's former lives. In these stories we read about how the Buddha developed the strengths he needed to become the Buddha over many lifetimes. Sometimes he was a human, sometimes an animal. In one story the Buddha is a hero called Prince Five Weapons, who had, as you may have guessed, mastered five weapons of immense power, guided by a great teacher of martial arts. The defining challenge of his life came in the form of a giant called Sticky Hair, who was terrorizing the countryside. No one could stop him, and so of course Prince Five Weapons took on the seemingly impossible.

Everyone was sure he could do it with his five great weapons. Yet he shot his arrows at Sticky Hair, and that didn't work; they just stuck in his hair. He shot poisoned arrows and threw his long sword, but no, everything got stuck. He tried to use his hands to punch the giant, but that didn't work either. There was something about his tenacity, though. Sticky Hair asked Prince Five Weapons, "Why aren't you afraid of me? Why aren't you afraid of death?" Sticky Hair was so impressed that he decided he didn't want to eat Prince Five Weapons right away.

Prince Five Weapons said to himself, "The five weapons given to me by my world-famous teacher have been useless. Even my lionlike strength has been useless. All the things I've learned from my teacher have failed me! I must go beyond my teacher and my body to what is inside my mind!"

He said to Sticky Hair, "My soft belly is a diamond that you can't digest."

Sticky Hair thought to himself, *No doubt this fearless man is telling the truth. I must not be able to digest him.* "In that case," he said, "I will let you go. You're a good man. I will not eat your flesh; I will let you go free like the moon that reappears after an eclipse so that you may shine pleasantly on all of your friends." What Prince Five Weapons learned was that what was inside of him was most valuable, and destroying Sticky Hair would only create more sorrow and suffering.

The prince said to Sticky Hair, "You have been born as a murderous, blood-sucking, flesh-eating demon. If you continue killing in this way, it will only lead to more suffering. You can only go from darkness to darkness this time." Sticky Hair became a student of Prince Five Weapons, and this giant began to live, knowing what peace is. He could've been shamed, or he could've fixated on his famed weapons not working, but instead he said, "Well, what's next?" Then he learned to do something new.

As we begin to think about these three giants, we have to be willing to meet them like the prince did, knowing that true strength is actually the softness in our belly. Paradoxically, that softness is like a diamond. As long as we remain grounded in ourselves, with a low sense of gravity and openness, we can be flexible and intelligent. When we clench up, tense up, go rigid, and fly out of our bodies, we become vulnerable to possession. To feel that softness in our bellies is to meet the giants directly, like my soft-bellied friend met the giant in the bagel shop.

When we move from a fighting posture to one of wisdom, then the giant will soften and listen to us. It may be our habitual identity that we can't deal with anger or with greed, when actually we can. We can learn how to train ourselves and practice doing something new.

THE GIANT OF GREED

We might think of the giant of greed as being like King Midas or Gordon Gekko from the movie *Wall Street*, but greed can take many different forms. It's not just greed for gold. It can be external or internal—for fancy cars, more cheesy pizza, a warm bagel, or the feelings we want: the good ones only, not the bad ones. It's an insatiability, like the hungry ghosts we talked about in chapter 2, our friends inside and outside us who never get enough. It comes from clinging to how we want to feel, what status we want to have, or what things we need to amass to protect ourselves from what we fear.

In the story of Hansel and Gretel, their mother conspires to have the children abandoned in the woods because she fears they can't feed them. Their father goes along with her fear, the desperate sense of "not enoughness." Hansel and Gretel grow up in this atmosphere. The mother forgets her own role as a protector of children, and the children become an object in a competition driven by a feeling of lack and the greed for what's left. Finally, she and the father cast out their own children into the woods. We do that, too. We cast out what we love when we're possessed. Nothing else matters; we can't even see our own loved ones. A common manifestation of that these days is our addiction to electronic devices. They become a propulsion into distraction, a greed for entertainment, and we are absorbed into our phones at every opportunity. It makes our partners and children feel invisible—which they actually are in those moments. We love our intimates, but we are propelled by compulsive dissatisfaction to be blind to these treasures right in front of us. The parents in the story of Hansel and Gretel can be seen as embodiments of this. They don't have enough, or they are afraid that in the next moment, the next day, the next month, they will not have enough. This becomes such an obsession that they cannot be satisfied today, the day they have with their precious children. This is like us far too often.

At first Hansel and Gretel are hip to this, and they can still find their way back to themselves, as symbolized by the trail of white pebbles they leave to find their way home. Eventually, though, they lose this sense of the way back home under the onslaught of their mother's feeling of lack and greed. One day they leave not marbles but a fragile trail of breadcrumbs representing their vanishing sense of themselves. It disappears, and they can't find their way back.

Their loss of home is the beginning of an adventure that is quite scary but also one in which they will find themselves. Many of us may have been brought up by parents who did not have a right relationship with the giant of greed. When it's not seen for what it is, we get possessed by it too. We get so hungry that we don't understand this giant, and we let the witch lure us into the house of candy. That's how we replay, generation after generation, the same kind of entrapment.

The children meet a witch, who tempts them to enter her domain with her fabulous candy-house, playing on their own greed, so that she can in turn consume them. The witch here is the archetypal pusher: the purveyor of addictive goods. This is the effect of greed intergenerationally. The children are entrapped and are being enslaved and consumed, but Gretel uses her wits to help them escape. She deals directly with the witch, like the monk eating the snake's head. She takes responsibility for where she is. She does this by pushing the witch into her own oven. She is no longer enslaved to the witch, who exploited the giant of greed inside Gretel. She frees Hansel, who was to be eaten, and the two of them discover a treasure inside the house. That treasure is nobility, a way to be honest about the role of addiction and greed in our lives and to meet it with honesty, responsibility, and skill. That's how we escape the witch's house, and when we get out, we leave it carrying the true treasure.

Reflection

What addiction is holding you in its hands? How are you trapped by greed in a way that consumes you or presses you into bad bargains? How can you find a way to outwit the witch inside you?

Releasing the tight grip is a place of practice.

THE GIANT OF ANGER

The negative effects of anger and resentment are easy to see. We lose our temper and do something we can't take back; we snap at our friend and immediately regret it; we say something too sharp to our child or parent or coworker. One day in the kitchen with Chodo, who was standing by the fridge listening to the radio, I needed to get into the fridge. Suddenly I found this beast in me, and I felt he had to move right now! It felt simply outrageous that he was there blocking the fridge so thoughtlessly! I needed to use it right now! The creature in me was suddenly swollen with anger. I could feel some unkind words starting to move my lips, and I thought, *Whoa, what's going on here?* I was feeling tired and wanted to get my breakfast together, and somehow his just being there felt so irrationally extreme, like I had to fight him, unleash something on him.

Now, all I had to do was to take hold of his hips and move them gently. He said, "Oh, sorry, I didn't realize you were trying to get into the fridge." Yet often we don't catch the beast. We unleash it as opposed to getting curious. Anger is a real giant in the human world, an elemental force that can cause mayhem and can bring justice. Everything depends on how it is held. That's one of the reasons why fairy tales are true emotionally, psychologically, and spiritually, like the giants in "Jack and the Beanstalk."

When Jack grew the beanstalk out of magic beans, he went into the territory of the giants and didn't have any curiosity about them as beings. Jack wasn't curious about the giants, and the giants were not curious about Jack. In that moment when anger arises, we can so easily lose our curiosity about who we are and who we are with. Unleash the kraken! When we're acting out of that space, possessed by our thoughts and feelings, we can become like our friend Angulimala. He was possessed by his fear and using the giant's energy without an intelligent relationship to it. There are times when rage is appropriate. Once it takes over, though, our intelligence and compassion go out the window.

When we have a mindful relationship to the giants, we can decide to show some anger, which is not the same thing as just unleashing it. On certain—usually rare—occasions, this is appropriate. Is it the right time to go into battle? If we see someone is going to be harmed, like when a parent uses their rage to yell at a child who is running into traffic, or when we need to speak fiercely to bring someone back to their wise selves, it can be the right thing to do. But what I felt in the kitchen was in no way that, not by a long shot. In that moment Chodo didn't fully exist; he was an object that needed to be dealt with, not the person I love. If we pay attention, we will see and admit that anger most often objectifies others, erasing their complex humanity.

Reflection

Call to mind someone you are angry with. Notice if when you think of them their humanity shrinks and they become an object—probably a repellent one, or an evil one. Try reintroducing some humanity, and see if you still feel it is appropriate to move toward them with anger. Imagine them as a child, as someone's baby. Imagine their suffering, their confusion, their limitations. You may still have a desire to address their behavior, but how does it feel now that you've introduced compassion into the mix?

Not holding on to anger is a place of practice.

RAHULA AND THE BEANSTALK

When the Buddha's son, Rahula, was seven years old he joined the community of monks and nuns and traveled with his father. The Buddha gave him two pieces of advice to guide his journey along the Eightfold Path. The first was to always tell the truth. The second was to watch, before, during, and after what he did, to see if his actions were for the happiness of himself and others or not.

But not Jack. "Oh, there's a beanstalk," Jack says, and he goes up. Going up to the realm of the giants, though, is that a good idea? You find yourself climbing into that realm, like I did in the kitchen. A thought or a feeling appears, like the beanstalk, and you climb it; you don't ask questions. The Buddha told Rahula we need to pause; we need to inquire. Through my work with incarcerated peoples, I learned the notion of "the moment before," the seconds before they crossed a line they thought they'd never cross. That monstrousness exists in all of us, and unless we're alert, it's just a matter of time until the right conditions come along to wake it up. In the case of those incarcerated individuals, they did something—or many things—that lasted mere moments, but their lives were forever changed. It's important to recognize this, and it's also important to have tenderness in our attitude and how we work with it. In order to admit the ridiculousness of what we're doing, we need a willingness to be uncomfortable. We have to give ourselves some space and tenderness to be fallible human beings.

How do we learn how to pause and ground when we feel angry or activated? I get really into my body, feel my feet on the floor, and feel the softness of my belly. If it's tight, I put my hands on top of each other just below my belly button, just being aware of the breath, allowing it to move my hands. If it's moving my hands, it's usually getting softer. Nothing fancy. Checking on my shoulders, opening them up, looking around, asking "Where am I?" Those help.

The Face of the Other

When we're angry, we're in some story. We can get curious. "Wow, what am I really angry about? What's really going on here? What is it made of? Is it my desire for control, my fear, is it injustice? Is it that somehow I or this other person wasn't listening? I didn't feel seen or received? What is it?" It's a challenging and wonderful place of inquiry. What's really going on? If we question deeply, we most often will walk away with some degree of increased compassion both for ourselves and others.

It's important to reflect on how we are perceiving those who are "making us angry." We can do this by grounding ourselves and then looking, really looking, at their face. This person also has a life, struggles, and suffering; is tangled up; and on some level wants to feel good. They may not know how to, but they want that. In the kitchen, when Chodo turned around and I could see his face, his eyes, his ears, and his cheeks, suddenly once again he was precious to me.

At the same time there are other people who we can't connect to that feeling. There is a person in my life who causes so much harm, seemingly totally unconsciously. They don't mean to cause harm. They don't wake up in the morning and decide to say mean things to make others feel miserable. It's a daily practice to recognize people's humanity and their commonality with us, to regard enemies or threatening people with compassion. Sometimes I need to say out loud to myself, "They're hurting too. They're causing harm, and they're hurting."

The practice, the nobility, is in the fulcrum: that space where instead of being carried along by the emotion, we can find clarity and the ability to shift. This willingness, this nimbleness, is something that we can learn over a lifetime: to be that fulcrum so that we do not get caught in one-sidedness. As my teacher Sensei Dai En Friedman says, "easy to say," especially if the person feels toxic or is causing harm. When those feelings of anger toward someone come up, I take a moment and reground and think, *They harm, and they are responsible for it, and yet I feel such tenderness when*

I think about how they must feel inside of themselves. That must not be so much fun.

THE GIANT OF DELUSION

We love to tell ourselves stories—about ourselves, about others, about anything and everything. The problems arise when we mistake these stories for truth and live in them. In this way, we make our stories real—they become a self-fulfilling and often self-defeating prophecy. How do we begin to see ourselves and reality more clearly?

Little Red Riding Hood was sent off to deliver some things to her grandmother, deep into the woods, and she was told to stay on the path. When she encounters the wolf, he is alone, which is not auspicious. In reality, the only reason a wolf is alone is that it is scouting or sick. The solitary aspect of the wolf is important— often, the lone wolf is a figure who is not well and caught in some idea. Little Red Riding Hood encounters the wolf and speaks to him naively, from that part of her that's not alert, that's not cautious about the potential for delusion. Like Jack, she just goes along with the story that's presenting itself. She doesn't understand she's going along with the way things appear to her, that this wolf is just like anyone, just normal. Red Riding Hood says, "I'm going to see my grandma, bring her some bagels," and the wolf asks where that is. All perfectly normal. We so easily get into this space where we don't stop to ask, "What is the situation here?"

The wolf says, "Go off the path, there's some beautiful flowers, it is so wonderful!" She doesn't ask herself, "Why is this wolf giving me a botanical tour?" She's caught in her distractedness and the way things appear to her, never mind that she's giving her grandmother's address to a wolf. There's no inquiry. This is the delusive nature of trusting our stories without checking them out.

So off she goes into the woods, and of course as we know the wolf then goes and eats the grandmother. Little Red Riding Hood goes to her grandmother's house, and she's caught too. She's so caught in how she wants things to be, or in the story she's fallen inside of. This is the way we are, building a life like hers in that moment, when we don't understand what's dangerous and we don't meet the reality of the present moment. What's dangerous? The way we lie to ourselves, and the way we believe the thoughts and feelings that possess us. We're seeing the world as though it's a projection screen.

Reflection

There's a beautiful Zen story where Nansen, a ninth-century Zen teacher, points to a peony in the garden and says, "These days people see these peonies as if in a dream." That was in medieval China; how much more so now! We see what we want to see or what we're afraid will happen, as opposed to what actually is. Can you think of a time in your life when you were so lost in a story—either a good one or a bad one—that you didn't see what was right under your nose?

Encountering life right now, as it is, is a place of practice.

Coming out of Delusion

When Little Red Riding Hood is swallowed by the wolf, it's not the end of the road for her. Someone kills the wolf and takes her out of it in this fantastic moment of magical realism—you know, she's totally fine, and so is Grandma. When the delusion is pierced and the bubble is popped, the world does become fresh and new again. Our delusion doesn't have to be the end. Our delusion can instead be a practice of getting down and back up again. My practice is learning how to deflate and reground, like we need to do with all of these giants. They might look like wolves, your parents, lovers, friends, but we can learn to ground and soften ourselves and come into a new reality.

THE THIRD NOBLE TRUTH

The third noble truth, the truth of nirvana, means we can change. The original meaning of nirvana related to "cooling" or "blowing out a painful fire." It also had the connotation of the liberation of awareness. When we untangle ourselves, we feel cooled and liberated. Fires may be burning, but we're not being consumed by them.

To begin this process of cooling and relief we must have a reckoning with our sorrow, tangles, discomfort, disease, awkwardness, and painful stories, and that's why we spent the last six chapters exploring these things and how we can discover we are more than them by ceasing to run from them.

Many of us want to jump onto the path and say, "From now on I'm going to be mindful, spiritual, happy," and ascend from there straight up into the sky of virtuous bliss, but that's not the way it works. We have to go through the knots, the swamps, and sometimes the wastelands. One of my students had a huge knot of yarn, and she decided to slowly untangle it as a practice, and part of her wanted to throw it out: *It's too difficult, it's too hard*. And then she would come back to it. *Okay, now, where does this piece go? Where does this one thread go?* It's these threads of our lives that are all tangled up in our delusions, rage, struggle, and suffering. These have to be breathed through, welcomed, and allowed to be part of the larger landscape.

Many of us just want to flee the house of self, run away, go toward the good stuff, run to the land of Rainbow Brite without dealing with our suffering. Yet that's not being real. Yes, we will go beyond the house of self, but first we have to take care of it. If we try to let go of the house of self while it's filled with debris, rickety, and falling down, with corners we haven't looked in for years, then even though we may have moments of ease and peace, we will also have moments of stepping in weird substances, springing forgotten mouse traps on our bare feet, and falling through rotting planks of wood. Our mind and body are our home, and even as we learn to stop limiting ourselves by believing that's all we are, we still need to take responsibility for our messes and lovingly care for the shape they're in.

We need to learn how to be real, and this sometimes means welcoming what we don't want to welcome. This is necessary in order to fully move toward real change. It takes a lot of effort, but it can be done.

Over every mountain there is a path, although it may not be seen from the valley.

—THEODORE ROETHKE

Without devotion any life becomes a stranger's story.

—MARIE HOWE

CHAPTER 7

The Pivot: Finding Our Place of Practice

Shunryu Suzuki once said, "After you have practiced for a while, you will realize that it is not possible to make rapid, extraordinary progress. Even though you try very hard, the progress you make is always little by little. It is not like getting into a shower in which you know when you get wet. In a fog, you do not know you are getting wet, but as you keep walking you get wet little by little. If your mind has ideas of progress, you may say, 'Oh, this pace is terrible!' But actually it is not. When you get wet in a fog it is very difficult to dry yourself. So there is no need to worry about progress."

As we begin to discuss turning the Dharma wheel and walking the path, keep that image in mind. My tradition, Soto Zen, is sometimes called "farmer Zen" because we value taking our time. The approach is gentle. When we develop slowly, patiently, and without hurry or ego trips about our "enlightenment," our progress is gradual but dependable.

The Buddha is known as the great physician because he

structured his teachings as a diagnosis—suffering—and a prescription, which is knowing our suffering and walking the Eightfold Path. To take the prescription, we have to know what our tangles are. We have to move into that gap and acknowledge the truth of our suffering and struggles. We have to meet the giants of our greed, resentment, and anger, and push through confused ideas.

ON HOPE AND ACTION

Hope is something important to reflect on. Many people consider hope a virtue, even a sacred principle, but it's a provocative fact that many of the world's wisdom traditions disagree about the nature of hope. Hope is the twin of fear, after all, and they go together. I'm struck by the myth of Pandora's box—or baskets, actually, in the original. In one version the gods gave Pandora one basket that was full of blessings and one full of plagues, and she was not to open them. She was so curious about what was in the plague basket. This is so like us—like when we want to watch a horror movie, or we slow down to look at road accidents. This attitude can sometimes get us into trouble.

Pandora opens up the basket, and greed and anger and ignorance and all of the terrors of humanity fly out. Just as she's about to close the lid on the basket, though, hope sneaks out. The thing is, though, that hope is a plague. Some even say hope is what makes the other things plagues at all. How is that? Hope is a wish for something different, but in a way that takes away our own agency. It's like waiting for the big babysitter to come and make everything right again. Hope is not action, and too often it can prevent action or even weaken us; when things don't turn out the way we hoped, we fall into despair or depression. Hope is not a strategy, and it's not doing the right thing for its own sake. If we're engaging in actions just because they're right—because they're beautiful—then whether we get what we want beyond those actions doesn't matter either. Freedom can look like acting because it is attuned to our values and wisdom, not for the sake of getting it right. Either way, hope has nothing to do with it.

When I think of facing the truth and taking action, I think of my ancestors, my great-grandparents, who knew that something terrible was coming in Eastern Europe and did something about it. They felt the tangle of what was happening in the world and were not deluded about it. They fled Ukraine, Hungary, and Poland, and everyone thought they were crazy for leaving. "That's not going to happen here!" they were told.

It's like the climate crisis. We have a dangerous tendency to think things are going to continue pretty much the way they've been already, and then when life surprises us, as it inevitably will, we are unprepared to meet it with our values. I imagine my ancestors being willing to listen to a growing feeling that things change, and that needs to be reckoned with. They were not fooled by wishful thinking. They left home and bounced around the world until they landed here, forced to migrate but following the impulse of life. It's essential to follow that impulse. What's life-giving? When we remain sensitized to that question, we can sense when we're living in the land of zombies and make a different choice.

Once we shift, we turn ourselves and see that there is a path, which does not avoid or deny suffering, which in many ways is this nobility that we've been exploring, the nobility of meeting reality straight up. We have the means to work with it, and we have the way beyond it, which is through it, and that is the path.

EXPANSIVE, NOT LINEAR

The path is not linear, just as life is not linear, even though we tell stories that make it seem like it is. When we tell stories of our own lives, they seem that way because we've chosen to arrange things to tell an explanatory story in time. We're never telling the whole story, though, because the whole story is not knowable. We don't really know what has been most important on our way, and we don't know all the causes and conditions that went into our story, not by a long shot.

When you walk into a planetarium, you get your ticket, you find your seat, the seats go a little bit back, maybe you're with someone else or maybe you're not, and then the projector goes on. Suddenly your problems, your ticket, your seat, and your morning coffee are nowhere. You zoom out, and suddenly there's a vast canopy of reality, solar systems, nebulae, other galaxies, black holes perhaps. It's amazing, and you start to see that this idea of a linear life doesn't seem to make sense anymore. That limited view just doesn't hold up. We exist in a massive, ungraspable web of causes and connections, and from our little peephole we construct a story that makes sense of what we've experienced. And as we probably know, those stories can change, sometimes drastically, with new information or understanding.

We can see that our simple stories are partial. We may need them to navigate, but we shouldn't hold them too tightly. We should allow them to be revised and evolve. If our stories of ourselves are not that trustworthy, what does that say about our stories about other people? Being humble about the fixed narratives we construct about our own lives can lead us to bring even greater humility to our stories about others.

How does this relate to the path? Well, as we set out on it, it's good to keep in mind that our understanding of what we're doing and of ourselves and others will change. The path is a way into mystery where we find both learning and a growing sense of how provisional our understanding of things is. This is not discouraging, though; it is a way into openness and carrying our stories lightly, the very things that allow us to grow slowly in some kind of wisdom.

Reflection

Think back on your earlier life and the way you understood yourself and others. See if you can call to mind how your understanding has evolved. Open yourself to the realization that the way you understand yourself and others now is also likely to change. Embrace this as a walk into an ever more expansive and refined understanding, with no end in sight.

Widening out is a place of practice.

Crossing the Line

When Chodo and I are training a group of physicians in contemplative medicine, we have an experiential lesson: Participants are asked to step over a line on the floor if they'd had a certain kind of experience. Have you lost a parent? A child? Been divorced? Had a brush with death? Had major surgery? Been assaulted? Gone bankrupt? Oh my goodness, what people have been through! What we've been through! We're all on this path together, and being on this path is possible because we all have these experiences. We isolate, and the isolation itself is what cuts us off; we think, *Oh, if other people really knew me, they would think I was weird. They would think whatever they would think. I am a weirdo, a freak.*

We ask participants to step over the line if they feel that their life is not integrated. Almost every time, everyone crosses the line. There are tears, and some people sob, because when we start opening up to the complexity of our shared human reality, we realize we're all in this together—people from all races, ethnicities, self-expressions, sexual orientations—and everyone has these human experiences of loss and love and trauma and pain, belonging and not belonging. We begin to see that our life is not so strange, that we can move forward together. Realizing this is another way to get out of our isolation. As the Buddha said, "Beautiful friendship is the whole of the spiritual life."

Reflection

Think of the people close to you. What tragedies, challenges, and losses have they experienced? Think of two or three of the most challenging things each one has faced. How does this make you feel about them? About your own challenges?

Not turning away from challenges is a place of practice.

Go Straight On

There's an old Zen story in which a group of monks are trying to find the way to Mount Gotai, and they stop in a tea shop to ask directions. They ask the old woman selling tea, and she says, "Go straight on." They start doing just that, going straight on, and she says, "Uh-oh, lost your way!"

So they tell their teacher, and the next day the teacher himself goes to see this nameless old woman. He asks her the way to Mount Gotai, and she says, "Go straight on." The teacher understands. She is talking about uprightness, not denying but fully inhabiting our lives.

I was raised by people who held many beautiful values like justice, equality, fairness, and diversity, and yet their actions often did not reflect those values at all. From early on I became interested in that gap, as children do. *How is it these wonderful people are doing or allowing terrible things to happen?*

When I was in high school our dear family friends, Michael and Gerry, got "gay cancer," before we knew it would be called HIV/AIDS, and we used to visit them in the hospital. I saw there how the doctors and nurses and social workers, people committed to lives of healing and service, nevertheless treated our friends so badly, because they were full of fear. What causes this gap? The Buddhist response is that without a path of practice it is difficult to narrow the distance between your values and your actual day-to-day living.

The fourth noble truth, that of the path, asks, "How do you fall down and get back up again?" When we realize we're not living freshly, not embodying the practice, and not on the path, it's how and with what attitude we get up that is so important, so critical. We can see in ourselves, in all walks of life, in all communities, everywhere, where we're not really connected, that we're avoiding or denying the reality of life.

TURNING THE WHEEL

Turning the Dharma wheel, as we'll explore throughout this book, is a way to untangle our perspective, thoughts, speech, behavior, work life, effort, paying attention, and focus. We say turning the wheel, but in some ways the wheel actually turns us. Many people before us have turned this wheel, and we benefit from their efforts. They turn the wheel, and the wheel turns us. We turn the wheel, and in so doing we turn the wheel for others. When we practice the eight parts of the path, they function together like the spokes of a wheel, and we move forward. Here's a snapshot of the terrain before we move on:

- **Perspective as a place of practice** means shifting from what has been done to me to "what I am doing." With regard to others, it means finding a way to compassion through facing our own suffering.
- **Intention as a place of practice** means asking the question, "How do I seek a happiness that doesn't involve exploiting other people or doing them harm?"
- **Speech as a place of practice** means speaking with reflection, generosity, and a resistance toward falling into the easy, habitual patterns of thoughtless or harmful speech. Words

have power. How are we using them when we talk to others as well as ourselves?

- **Action as a place of practice** means getting in touch with our values and being clear about what those are. You've heard the saying "the road to hell is paved with good intentions"; this is because our actions are our true belongings. They are a clear indicator of whether we are walking the walk and not just talking the talk.

- **Work as a place of practice** means having some consciousness in our livelihood, in our work, and not separating it from our values or our mindfulness, because one-third of our lives is spent at work.

- **Effort as a place of practice** means we have to make a good effort. As Rainer Maria Rilke wrote, "It's hard." It's hard to change, to stay steady, to have a creative and vital life. How we summon the energy for change and transformation is a place of practice.

- **Attention as a place of practice** means cultivating the kind of focus and presence that allows real change. The path itself is in the midst of the gap, in the tension of that gap, between our values and what we actually think, say, and do. It's a life of living with curiosity and awareness and paying attention is the ground of it.

We're not ever going to actually get good at it, but the willingness is everything—or as meditation teacher Ajahn Chah says, how much you put into it is equal to your own level of freedom. What I learned from Sensei White is that if we pay attention, we can develop that concentration. I can feel afraid, or that I want to get the hell out of here. I can feel awkward, nervous, ashamed, any of that, and stay with it, stay in relationship with my community, in the grocery store or the coffee shop or the gym. Once we have this concentration, we can have this different sense of awareness.

Finally, we come to what's often thought—rightly or wrongly—to be the heart of Zen, which is seated meditation, or zazen. We'll talk about how to cultivate this essential practice and let it become the ground of our lives, a space of freedom where we can receive and enjoy the raw experience of ourselves and our life with stability and expansiveness. Delicious.

PART III

~⌒~

THE EIGHTFOLD PATH TO CLARITY, COURAGE, AND COMPASSION

To greet sorrow today does not mean that sorrow will be there tomorrow. Happiness comes too, and grief, and tiredness, disappointment, surprise and energy. Chaos and fulfilment will be named as well as delight and despair. This is the truth of being here, wherever here is today. It may not be permanent but it is here. I will probably leave here, and I will probably return. To deny here is to harrow the heart. Hello to here.

—PADRAIG O TUAMA

CHAPTER 8

The Path Is a Place of Practice

Many people think Buddhism is simply about feeling peaceful and "getting your Zen on." In actuality, hiding out in a frozen trance is known in Zen as being a "dead tree" or being "lost in the demon cave." Zen is about non-grasping, which results in a mind that is flexible and vital. This can only happen when you're not hypnotized. The fundamental shift which is the actual essence of Zen is *taking responsibility for what we're doing in the present moment*. Taking responsibility in this way is something that many of us really don't want to do. It's scary, but it's the road to freedom.

PERSPECTIVE

The first of the eight aspects of the Eightfold Path is that of perspective. Its essence is a deliberate move from "what has been done to me" to "what I'm doing to me, and what I can do differently."

When I was studying with John Daido Loori Roshi, I and some other students got stuck in a trap of waiting passively for the teacher to do our work for us. We wanted the teacher to be so perfect, so charismatic, so perceptive, that they would sweep us up and ferry us right to nirvana. Daido Roshi was not interested in pulling any such Wizard of Oz trick, and we were disappointed. We became full of criticism: They were not correct and not giving what they should be giving. I was so young, twenty years old, and I was hoping this teacher and this path would save me from my struggle. Given my background, I was prone to reactivity and easily triggered due to trauma. I felt constantly under threat. I was a little crazy coming from my background, and I'd been so traumatized, so under threat. I wanted this particular community and teacher to fix all of that. That meant them doing the work of operating on me and taking all of that stuff out. It didn't mean them throwing me back to rely on my own resources and giving me the inspiration and the support to do the hard, painful work myself.

Looking back, Daido Roshi was in fact always clear about what they were there to do, which was to support people in experiencing their own capacity to wake up. It's not anyone's job to wake someone else up. I had fallen in with this critical group who were more interested in whether or not the teacher and community were what they *should* be in their opinion than they were in their own practice. I wasn't even aware of how passive I had become with regard to my present-moment practice and how aggressive I had unconsciously become toward the teacher. I was hypnotized by this strategy of evasion.

Checking Our Pockets

There's a great story told by Paul Breiter in his book about his time studying with Ajahn Chah, called *Venerable Father*. There was a

Western monk named Aranyabho, who was wandering from monastery to monastery, always dissatisfied. One day, when Breiter sat down to talk with Ajahn Chah, the master said, "Aranyabho's got dogshit in his pocket. He goes somewhere and sits down but there's a bad smell, so he thinks hmmm, this place is no good. He gets up and goes somewhere else, but he notices the bad smell again so then he goes somewhere else...He doesn't realize he's carrying the dogshit around with him wherever he goes."

For many years I treated the world as it was when I was a child—unsafe, untrustworthy. I didn't belong anywhere, and that's just how it was. That was the shit in my pocket. In every group I joined I would find problems after a couple of years—it was so repetitive. Jon Kabat-Zinn says, "Wherever you go, there you are." You're bringing your shit everywhere. Wherever you go, that's where the shit lands.

Right Perspective

When we take up right perspective, we start to understand that it is *our* actions we need to focus on. It's our doings, our thoughts, our words that have consequences. Many times people go on long retreats, and when they come back, they get so pissed off with the imperfections and demands of their family, their boss, their pets that they lose their mindfulness and peace. We are grasping at good things, yes, but even so we can become these little demons. In Japanese folk culture, there are little demon creatures called onis. They are not good or bad, and yet they often cause havoc. When we are grasping, we can feed these onis without thinking. That's not taking responsibility for what we're doing in the present moment, which is the real leverage we have and the beginning of the path. As we're entering this first fold of the path of nobility, the essence is to take our seat, realize it's our seat, and take responsibility for ourselves. Right perspective can also be translated as "right view." This doesn't refer to view in the sense of a doctrine or body of beliefs, but rather is a combination of attunement and vision. It's attuned seeing. There's research about actual vision and what happens when we're racked with anxiety and fear. When that happens, your pupils literally tighten up and your vision gets small. Learning how to widen out and how to rest in the softness of your belly helps us to be in this attuned view of things. When our vision is attuned, every moment, person, and thing can be a teacher.

Reflection

Is there a place in your life where you are focusing too much on what is happening to you and not enough on what you are bringing to the situation? If you could bring something different, what would it be?

Shifting is a place of practice.

BUT WHAT AM I DOING?

Recently I was at a business meeting where people were being critical about something, and I found myself overidentifying with what they were criticizing (which was not me), but I still got worked up and had a lot of reactive feelings. Have you ever had that experience? Rather than observing my feelings, I started to speak *from* my feelings. This was deeply unskillful and caused some harm to some people, and I was responsible for that.

It is a nobility of view to see how it's not just what people are doing to you, what life is doing to you, or what your thoughts, actions, words are doing. How did that incident feel? For me, it felt yucky. That yuck moment is so important. Earlier in my life, I would feel that and push it down, or the question in my mind would be, "Who is making me feel that way?" I would go back to that reactivity and habit energy of blaming and feeling ashamed rather than healthy embarrassment. Our lives begin to transform when we shift our attention to what we ourselves are doing in the present moment.

The Grandmotherly Mind

We might think, *I'm a caring person; ain't that enough?* And yet, care without contemplation of our own actions is not really care. To live a caring life requires contemplation—that inward look—for the sake of how we are in relation to other people. We watch, but we do it with what, in the Zen tradition, we call a "grandmotherly mind." We should not underestimate how powerful that grandmotherly mind is. Grandmotherly mind has perspective. Have you ever watched a kid misbehaving in the presence of their parents and their grandparents? Often the parents will react with some uptightness, with identification and embarrassment, whereas the grandparents may have a different perspective and not take it so seriously—they still respond and offer guidance, and yet sometimes it's given with good humor and compassion. The anthropologist

Kristen Hawkes has suggested that it may have been due to living with grandmothers that humans were able to evolve in the way we were—and maybe that's part of the reason why. That expansive mind, that generational mind, can look at the big picture and hold us with kindness and forgiveness while giving us a little nudge to do what's right.

SUFFERING IS UNIVERSAL

Another way to shift focus from what is being done to us to what we are doing is remembering how universal the experience of suffering is. As the Buddha said, everyone experiences harsh words and blame, and everyone experiences stress, suffering, lamentation, and despair. Everyone experiences aging, sickness, and death. To illustrate this, one of the most famous stories of early Buddhism is that of Kisa-Gotami. Kisa-Gotami's son dies in infancy, and she is so overwhelmed by grief that she refuses to accept the reality and goes wandering in a crazed state, still holding his swaddled body. She keeps asking people for medicine for her sick baby. Someone tries to help her by sending her to the Buddha, who tells her he can help her with her son's "condition" if she can bring him a mustard seed from a house where no one has ever died. Kisa-Gotami heads off optimistically to find that house, but as she goes from door to door, she begins to realize the truth and receive the Buddha's intended message. There is no such house. She comes to accept the reality of her son's death.

That story has so much medicine in it. We shouldn't overlook the importance of Kisa-Gotami having gone from door to door listening to other people's stories. That's what she had to do to be able to open up beyond her own pain. In house after house, she hears the story of what happened to them, she hears these stories of grandmas and uncles and aunts and babies dying. Imagine what it would be like if she came to your door, this woman carrying a dead child and asking for mustard seeds. It's poignant that people receive her and no one turns her away, they tell her their stories of sorrow and struggle, and ultimately she realizes that everyone experiences loss. Her "why me" and her "this can't be happening" disappear. Recognizing the reality of our collective experience of pain, loss, disappointment, and sorrow is important.

For a few months I was working with a family whose father died of pancreatic cancer. His partner and the two teenage kids were bereft. For the beginning of our work, we just allowed the howling of the pain of the loss. We listened together of the stories of their dad waking them all up on the weekends with Joni Mitchell blasting. "Time to wake up sleepyheads," he would say as he danced around from room to room. His partner shared how he always held their face before he left to go anywhere. Tender moments. They all ached for him. The family had a tight-knit circle of friends and family, and I began to ask them if they knew what it was like for their loved ones when they lost someone dear. They said, "Great question." Over dinners, they began to open conversations with the families about their grandparents, aunts, uncles, and cousins who had died. Their circle started to knit together in a new way. Loss and grief were things all the adults and all the kids had experienced. Near the end of our time together, one of the teenage boys turned to me and said, "Koshin. You know what my dad taught me? Our suffering is universal, and so is love."

Questioning Our Thoughts

We are in a pandemic of loneliness. We can get hijacked by our own social isolation and keep feeding it. Loneliness is an insatiable creature. By learning how to widen out and knock on the doors of our own mind and of the world, we can inquire more deeply and ask, *Is that thought really true?* Many of our thoughts are paper tigers and fold under a little pressure. We're intimidated by them, but if we question them, they will fall apart surprisingly easily. Like a good journalist who wants to get as much—possibly damning—information as possible from the person they are speaking to, we can act naive, and we keep on asking questions. "Why do you think that? Oh, and is that true? And what will happen then? And why does that matter?" The thoughts that make us suffer so often make no sense, and calling their bluff will many times make them vanish. The next time you are troubled by anxiety or anger, play dumb and ask those thoughts some naive questions. Keep on asking until they're stumped and give up the game.

Connecting inside and out is a place of practice.

WIDENING THE CIRCLE

To work with this nobility of view is to actually take up the trouble, what John Lewis called "good trouble," which means taking our most cherished assumptions about this world into some rigorous questioning. For example: How do you feel about yourself?

How do you feel about your mind, your social location, your sexuality, your gender? How do you feel about the cosmos?

You know what's amazing? Every single human being has a close and personal relationship with those things too. On the one hand, we can know our suffering, our giants of greed, anger, and delusion. On the other hand, we can see the way we all share these human realities. Although the emphasis in right perspective is on waking up to what we're doing in the present moment, this is not something we do alone. Our Zen community has people from all over, from different continents, from the other side of the equator. This means that you can say it's hot today, but for some people it's winter, or you can say good morning, but for some people it's the middle of the night. This may seem banal, but it often reminds me to get out of my own little experience. As I write, it is a hot summer on the island of Manhattan in New York, and that's not the whole story; that's just my little experience. Part of the work of right perspective is seeing that I'm totally responsible for what I do and that my experience, my suffering, is not the whole story.

Your Enemy

Our friends are not the only helpers on the path. Sometimes our enemies can help us even more. By "enemy" here I mean people who really get your goat and push your buttons. These can be great teachers. There is a story about the spiritual community led by G. I. Gurdjieff in France. One member of the community was a difficult old man. He was irritable and messy, always fighting with other people, and unwilling to do his share of the work. Nobody liked him, and he did not like the group.

After many months of struggling to stay with the group, the old man left for Paris. Gurdjieff went after him and tried to get him to come back, but the old man said no, it had been too hard. Finally, Gurdjieff offered to pay him a large monthly stipend if he returned, so the old man agreed. When the rest of the people heard that Gurdjieff was paying this miserable old cuss to stay in the community, when they themselves were being charged a handsome fee to be there, they were up in arms.

Gurdjieff called them together and said, "Look, without this man you would never really learn about anger, irritability, patience, and compassion. That is why you pay me, and I hire him."

___

Reflection

The next time you feel you have been treated unfairly, take a moment to yourself and breathe into your belly until it softens. Shift your perspective from what is happening to you to what you are bringing to the table yourself. What are you focusing your attention on? Are you focusing on the details of what happened with a sense of grievance or anger? Ask yourself if any of the ways you are attending and talking to yourself are causing suffering. If the answer is yes, ask yourself, "Is that really needed?" If it isn't, let it go. Make room for a response that is about positive change, not payback or just venting frustration.

Attention is a place of practice.

ATTUNING OUR VISION

I remember my grandma saying, "Boy, people get worked up, and for what?" This was her attunement to what's really important. Right perspective is being sensitive in the moment to how we are working ourselves up beyond what is given directly in our experience. Right perspective is a little like an internal cop who asks for "just the facts, ma'am." The facts mean parsing out what is directly given to us and, more importantly, what we are adding in the moment.

When someone says something to us, for instance, there are just words landing in our ears. Everything else is interpretation, which might be more or less accurate, but it's in that interpretation that we have power. Even if the words are objectively nasty, there is still a big difference between a wise interpretation, such as "speaking nastily is their problem, not mine" and "those nasty words are an existential threat to me, and I must make sure they are never spoken again." The first interpretation lets us disengage and then choose an intelligent response. The second one sends our amygdala into overdrive and signals that the internal movie we may be watching for the next several hours will either be the story of why that person is an evil bastard or the story of how I fucked up and made things much worse.

Views

I can hold cherished opinions and preferences and then build a world with those that excludes others. I wanted to meet this directly, so I thought, *What group do I feel like I have nothing in common with?* So, I created a practice where every morning I log on to a *very* white supremacist website. It's such an amazing practice because it takes me half a second to find myself equally rigid as these folks in my views, totally fixated on how wrong they are. These are the same people who were in Charlottesville, Virginia, in August 2017 rallying at the Unite the Right Rally with tiki torches, feeling so sure that they were right. The intolerance that shows up in me, that is not the medicine; it's just more of the same. The Buddha taught that one of the fetters that entangle us human beings is "clinging to views." This doesn't mean you don't have views—you do have views that you think are true and beneficial. Clinging, though, is the rigidity, the emotional charge, the subtle violence roiling beneath our social media arguments. I was at a peace rally where people were shoving and yelling, and the energy was so aggressive. This hostility, this sureness—that is not an attuned view of what we're doing, but an overfocusing on views, not the right view of attuned vision.

Reflection

What activities nourish your heart, not just in theory but in practice? Gardening? Dancing? Volunteering at the soup kitchen? Meditating? Reading Zen books? Playing an instrument? Talking to friends? Identify two and determine (on determination, see below) to make time for them this week.

Getting clear is a place of practice.

Great Doubt, Great Faith, and Great Determination

In Zen we talk about "great doubt, great faith, and great determination," which are the three pillars of practice according to the sixteenth-century master Torei Enji Zenji. These three qualities are also important for understanding right perspective. Great faith is in your own experience of what actually is nourishing and what supports you. This might not be what you normally think of as faith, but in fact it is easy to become disconnected from your deepest experiences of what is true and right. You need to have faith in them. People will tell you not to rely on that experience, to rely instead on money or fame or self-care perfectionism or whatever. You need to stay in touch with what really nourishes your heart and remind yourself of what that is every day.

Great doubt, for me, means doubting that the way I habitually tend to do things is correct. We need to be rigorous about our assumptions and opinions. To carry "great doubt" is not to settle for easy certainties or think that our learning is complete. It is realizing our understanding alone is never complete.

Great determination is so important because the practice does take effort. When we're battered by the winds and waves, we need to have determination to hold on, to reconnect with our great faith, to keep on finding joy. That's what you're trying on: great faith, doubt, and determination. You're attending to what you yourself are doing, questioning your assumptions, and trying that on.

That's learning to make our way out of the house of sorrow—our clinging, our biases, our fixations. When we ground ourselves beyond our "selves," learning to rest in our seats with soft bellies and realizing, as my dharma sister Chimyo Atkinson says, "No one else can teach you how to belong to the world."

What does it mean to belong to the world? It means nothing other than taking responsibility for your actions moment by moment. When Taizan Maezumi Roshi, the founder of the White Plum Soto Zen lineage in the United States, was meeting with students, one student, Egyoku Nakao Roshi said, "I'm going to do things my way; I don't like doing things your way anymore." Taizan Maezumi Roshi sat there quietly and said, "Just be careful on your way." The truth is that all of us are only on our own way, and things can be no other way. That is good and natural. We just need to be careful on our way.

The evil that is in the world always comes of ignorance, and good intentions may do as much harm as malevolence, if they lack understanding.

—ALBERT CAMUS

If you surrendered to the air, you could ride it.

—TONI MORRISON

CHAPTER 9

Perspective Is a Place of Practice

In the oldest texts, right intention is said to have three aspects: giving up our obsession with feeding on people and the pleasures of the senses, giving up ill will, and giving up causing harm. Untangling our intentions means asking, "How do I seek a happiness that doesn't involve exploiting myself and other people or doing them or me harm?"

When I started practicing more seriously, I went to Zen Mountain Monastery, which is where I started with Daido Roshi. I thought I was hardcore, really giving myself to the practice. My form was perfect; I prided myself on how I was engaged in disciplined, embodied practice. Yet my practice was really "outside in"; it didn't reach the heart. I used to sit in zazen deciding how I could be so clever that when I went to meet with the teacher, I would impress them so much that they would give me a cookie.

HUNGRY GHOSTS, COOKIES, AND TAKING RESPONSIBILITY

These cookies weren't the freshly baked kind. These cookies represented how I wanted everyone to respond to me, which was to like me, to think I was bright and creative and dynamic and full of possibilities. This pattern of seeking security in manipulating others' perceptions was what I felt kept me safe when I was a child. I was not aware of how I was enacting that again, thinking my intentions were merely to be a serious Zen student. In reality, I was like Cookie Monster, a big creature, shoving cookies in my mouth, shouting, "Cookies, cookies, cookies!" There was an obsessive quality to it; there was the idea of pleasure but no real pleasure. I wanted to rest and belong, but I didn't know how to do that, not even how to belong to my own body. I would be sitting in a beautiful meditation hall, in a seemingly idyllic meditative place, but what I was experiencing was the hungry ghost realm, those unexplored places inside are where the hungry ghosts breed.

I was not clear about what my intentions were. When a gap exists between how we want to be and feel and how we're actually working with our thoughts, it tends to cause havoc. I wanted to feel like I belonged and feel at rest and at ease in my own body and mind. But these runaway hungry ghosts were overriding my best intentions. It was very confusing to me. I kept reacting when I wasn't getting my cookie, as opposed to learning how to see my reactions and stopping and coming back to my breath and my belly. It was skewing my own ability to touch any kind of wisdom. Daido Roshi was not a cookie giver, so of course I thought he was an asshole. I ended up leaving the community with other people who felt that they weren't getting the cookies they wanted either. There was a little band of un-cookied people. We were like, "Yeah, we're going somewhere else." As the great Thai master Ajaan Lee once said, "Those who don't realize what the shadows of virtue are will end up riding only in the shadows."

We can band together in our skewed ideas like that. Then our hungry ghosts can all work together! Cookies are so delicious but not that good for you, as we all know.

We un-cookied individuals started a new community, but there I experienced the same pattern. It was still alive in me, but now I started to see it. During the early years of that new group, Mae-zumi Roshi came to visit. This was after some explosive news was revealed from the Zen Center of Los Angeles—Maezumi Roshi had been struggling with alcoholism and had slept with some of his students.

As the effects of these revelations spread, I found myself intrigued by the way Maezumi Roshi responded. He had entered treatment and was taking full responsibility, without justification or defense, for everything he had done. He was the first adult I had known who took responsibility for his actions like that. He never defended what he did; he simply said, "I have caused harm, a lot of harm, and I'm responsible." When I heard about that I felt such a deep love for him; I understood that you can make terrible mistakes, cause harm, and you can get back up. Maezumi Roshi never stopped practicing. His renunciation, his manifestation of right intention, was coming into the zendo each morning for the morning sit. He would open it up after the sit and anyone could say anything to him. People cried with him, people screamed at him, people sat in silence, and he did this, he just held the space and did not defend himself. I felt like that was a superpower, and something I had never experienced: "Yes, I did that. Tell me how it impacted you. I'm here, and I can receive it." How many people do you know who embody this form of courage?

His renunciation was about atonement, in the sense of

at-one-ment, becoming one with what you've done, not resisting it. His thought around his own taking responsibility was to be at one with what he had done. I know many people who caused harm like he did in many different contexts, and rarely is there someone who meets their wrongdoing like he did.

When he visited our center, he gave a Dharma talk about harmony and created a little calligraphy of the character *wah*, which means "harmony," that he left behind for us. I remember sitting there and thinking, *Wow, he is showing a path*. He had a big gap and he is closing the gap. He was a deeply wise and compassionate and flawed human being, like everybody, and yet he was totally dedicated and had a deep, deep love for the practice. Watching the way he dealt with the destruction of everything I was trying to create—perfect external form, charisma, wisdom, a total Zen personality—I not only saw that was he still practicing despite that explosion, but I saw that real practice was beyond those things I equated with practice, those things I was so busy trying to get cookies for.

It was during his talk, watching him so in his body, so alive, that it felt like through his transgression and atonement and continuous practice I was seeing a gate to how to be different, how to change, how to practice right intention. You can feel in someone's body whether they are really available or not, whether they are slinking away. "I'm not good enough," so many of our bodies say. "I did terrible things." Maezumi Roshi's body was saying, "Yes, I did terrible things" and not slinking away.

Maezumi was not exploiting and not manipulating; he wasn't denying reality or "handling the situation." He was living in the reality of what he did and the reality of how it had impacted others, being who he was as he was. That's one part of right intention: living in your life as it is, in your body as you are, and giving up arranging our lives as a manipulation of others in order to get cookies.

I noticed how I was treating other people as objects to manipulate to get what I wanted when I was caught up by my hungry ghosts. When we are obsessed with feeding on other people—their feedback, their opinions, their reactions—other people don't fully exist for us. They are just objects. It's like Leonard Cohen sings in the song "Treaty": "I'm sorry for the ghost I made you be. Only one of us was real, and that was me." This is something we're always going to have to be on the lookout for; we're never going to be done with it. I don't want to mislead anyone into thinking that even I am done! Yet this is something we can wake up to and have the intention to renounce.

Looking back, I'm sorry that I didn't know what it meant to have a teacher. I didn't fully allow Daido Roshi in. Now I appreciate the students who stick around long enough to allow both of us to be real. Often, I hear stories of marriages and friendships where you can feel that it's not really a relationship with the person; it's a relationship with ghosts, and we're acting "as if." That's not being real about our intentions in the moment.

Reflection

What are you doing to get a cookie? Try refraining from seeking cookies for one week, no matter what, and see if the supreme meal of life as it is can enter.

Pausing is a place of practice.

FIREFLIES IN THE DARK

One night I was biking home along the beautiful Hudson River, a bit later than I normally do. It was getting dark, and there is one part of the path that leaves the riverside and goes into a more wooded area. It was dark, and I was seized by this terrible fear. It came so intensely, and I felt unsafe and frightened. I felt cornered, and it reminded me of those nights in the bathroom as a child. Something was triggering that association, and suddenly I was careening into that neighborhood in my brain. At that moment I said to myself, "You can do this," and I brought my attention into my belly and breathed through it. It was so magical that a moment later I was able to notice that in the darkness the fireflies had come out. What had seemed scary and dark revealed these bursts and beams of light flickering everywhere inside it.

Finding the Glimmers

When we're running scared, the darkness is always right behind us, just out of view, and we can't find the glimmers of light inside of it. Sometimes there are no glimmers of light, of course, and then we have to let the darkness pass over us, but at least then we can get to the other side. Running, being hunted, is no way to live. When the darkness finally came for Maezumi Roshi, he faced it, and in that very facing created light for himself and others out of failure, harm, and loss. In my early years of Zen practice, I thought I was engaging in good practice, but I was actually just cooking up a facsimile in order to get cookies. That was, of course, an alternative to facing the darkness I was afraid of and beginning the process of growing up.

In the *Mumonkan*, an ancient Chinese collection of Zen teaching stories, there's one in particular about a monk named Zuigan who could call to himself every day, "Master!" and answer, "Yes, sir!"

Then he would say, "Are you awake?" and answer, "Yes!"

"From now on, don't be deceived!"

"No, I won't!"

We need to do that for ourselves. When we cultivate an awakeness to our intentions, we can begin to truly trust ourselves. Then, perhaps, we can have some tenderness.

ILL WILL

Ill will is usually thought of as wishing ill on people, but it's broader than that. It can also mean being averse to situations or to the way our experience feels right now. We can have ill will toward ourselves for being a certain way—most people I know and work with have that struggle inside of themselves.

Ill will can be directed toward our current experience or even feel like it is directed toward life itself. When this happens, we can practice noticing how things change. If the mind is freezing everything in place as being horrid, we can actively pay attention to how things are actually changing moment to moment. Instead of blanketing everything and painting it black, how do you get curious about what the day will bring? The simplest thing? Don't feel ill will toward your ill will. That can easily lead into a depressive spiral. Accept the fact that you're feeling ill will and it may be around for a while. Then pay attention to the details of the moment: how the air feels, how your feet feel touching the ground, the feeling of the clothes against your body, the way your breath changes. Your ill will is not the only thing going on, and in fact not everything you are experiencing is unpleasant. At times this can help unfreeze your mood and allow change.

Coming to Terms

Ill will can also be based in our worldview, something that seems as ubiquitous as COVID-19—or more. Cultivating right intention means coming to terms with how we hate. In this sense it doesn't matter what side of anything we're on. Ill will is the idea that the problem has to be eviscerated and destroyed. Ill will and obsession are good friends. It's so easy to get caught up in being right and dehumanizing the other. It's related to a sense of entitlement, projection, and objectification. We may also feel subtly guilty for being angry, and then dig our heels in even more to justify the fact that we're upset. All of this takes us out of reality and solves nothing. This is explained well by a story about two monks traveling along a road. They see a young woman trying to cross a stream, and one of them offers to carry her across. Afterward, one of the monks criticized his companion for having touched a woman. The monk explains why he did so—out of compassion—yet a few days later the monk brings it up again. His companion says, "I put her down days ago. Why are you still carrying her?" Ill will is like that kind of entrenchment. It's not just about the event and our feeling toward it—it's the mental replay that can go on for minutes, hours, or days.

Glimmers of Love

When we freak out about people who represent to us what threatens us (like when we exclaim, "The problem in American society today is _____!"), we're not neutrally addressing things; we're obsessed by fear and anger, and expressing that under the guise of making things better.

I recently acknowledged that every time I came across a certain person, I experienced a feeling of aversion and irritation. The best response was to focus on my breath, which is always a good idea, and then to be mindful of how I was thinking. How we think is the ground for our words and actions. To calm myself down, I then thought about how the person was struggling just the same as I was. This prompted curiosity and compassion. They probably had something—maybe a lot of something—in their life that was not so easy. I began to soften back into my own body and remember that when someone behaves so reactively, it's usually not exactly a party in their own head.

For this specific person I simply had to keep doing that, and I feel like those people are exactly the people who can teach us the most, like the difficult old man in Gurdjieff's group. Those are the people who can teach us the medicine for ill will, how to come back to our right intentions, how to come back to the nobility of our intention. When I did this, more tenderness slowly arose. This is meeting my own ill will with nobility, and from that comes softness and receptivity and even glimmers of love.

Lick the Honey

Have you heard the story about the person who was running from a tiger and fell down a well? He catches hold of a solitary branch sticking through the wall of the well. He's hanging there with a tiger above him and the far distant bottom of the well below him. He notices a mouse beginning to gnaw on the branch he's holding on to. Suddenly, a drop of honey falls from a hive built atop the well and lands on the branch. What does he do?

He licks the honey. It's delicious.

Take the lick of honey wherever it is. Even in moments of desperation, if there is honey around, take a lick. This is like finding fireflies in the dark. You could be stuck and feel bad about experiencing fear, but there is also a joy in experiencing what's right in front of you. What's beauty? It's paying attention. When you pay attention, you can find beauty in an ICU room. I have.

NON-HARM

Taking responsibility for our impact in the world is an essential place of practice. Non-harming is another way to look at our intentions. Are we causing harm, intentionally or unintentionally? The intention of non-harm is to be sensitive to whether our actions are causing harm, and to take responsibility for the harm we cause. I have a friend who, whenever they reflect on their actions, tends to skewer themself on how whatever they did was not quite right. You can feel the scrunching of their face as they think of themself—under the guise of "reflection"—and they are harming themself. There is a big difference between a rigorous way of working with our intentions and emotions, and harmful, obsessive self-punishment. There has to be careful attention to attunement, like turning a dial; we have to ask, is it the right pressure? Is it kind? Having the intention of non-harm with regard to others and the world is not enough. The truth is, the intention of non-harm begins with how we treat ourselves in the way that we think, the choices we make, what we take on in our lives. If we can recognize the harm we're causing ourselves and stop, this will naturally flow into harming others less too.

Breaking through Harmful Thinking

Recently I spoke with a friend whose reflections on themself skew a bit negative. They were thinking about something they had shared in a meeting we had both attended, and they felt bad about it even though the sharing had, in my opinion, actually been brave and healthy. They were shaming themself for behaving a certain way in the meeting, though all they had done was share their vulnerability. The next day they had a shame attack—the revenge of their defensive boundaries. When something like this happens, we need to learn how to pause and reflect, come back into the belly, and say, "My goodness, I'm hurting myself."

When the Buddha talked about the wheel of suffering, he was talking about all the compulsive, repetitive realms of being we create with our thoughts to hurt ourselves. Most of us think habitually. The brain is deeply repetitive. My friend was grinding herself down in a cruel way with this wheel, and she was divorced from the actual reality of what had happened—which is that she had been courageous. I asked her, "The way you're thinking seems to be harmful. Is it?" She was taken aback, and she said, "Yes, it really is." She began to cry. It was a relief to recognize that. Her thoughts were not defending her, they were hurting her.

I said to her, "Let's reflect on who was at that meeting yesterday and what might have invited you to share," and it turned out that everyone at that meeting had lots of capacity and groundedness and real care about her and are interested in what's real. She said, "Maybe that's what brought it out; I was in an environment that welcomes realness. It's so rare. I'm not used to it, but I sure am used to beating the shit out of myself."

Being received with loving attention in the midst of struggle can be powerful and important. In a small way I was able to do that for her, and it reminded me of how much we all need this. If we have a friend who can do this for us, that's wonderful, and if not, then we need to learn how to listen to our intentions with a grandmotherly mind.

Reflection

Are there stories or thoughts you use to beat yourself up? What are they?

Today, watch your thoughts, and see if you can notice any thoughts that hurt. If they hurt, ask yourself if you need to think them. Maybe you don't. Try letting them go. If it turns out you don't need them, why think them?

Non-harming is a place of practice.

The Nobility of Intention

I have a friend who used to be one of the owners of a celebrated restaurant, a man of incredible dignity and beauty, who teaches etiquette. He shared a story with me and Chodo about a rude customer who was talking loudly, saying terrible things and disturbing other people. I asked him how he worked with his own mind before he dealt with him. He said, "I was so embarrassed for him; he wasn't able to understand the harm he was causing, the agitation, the disturbance, and I felt strong enough to take on his embarrassment."

So non-harming is not just how we are to ourselves and others, but how we respond to others when they are causing harm. This is a path of freedom and nobility, not just a cookie path. The nobility of intention is to be alive in every moment, particularly when we're under stress or duress or being harmed. That aliveness means not shutting down, not looking for cookies, and not taking revenge. It means staying alive to the humanity of everyone involved.

THE GREAT PACIFIC GARBAGE PATCH

The Great Pacific Garbage Patch is located between Hawaii and California. It is estimated to contain about 1.8 trillion plastic pieces totaling eighty thousand tons, the weight of five hundred jumbo jets. We are aware of this, yet we still use plastic. This plastic patch embodies all of our intentions, our skewed intentions, personified. Many of us feel that if it is out of sight, it is out of mind. In some ways our entire culture is built around that idea: Toilets flush human waste away; garbage trucks ferry our refuse to a faraway location.

How do we begin to see that everything in the world is connected, that we are connected to what happens out in the world?

We feel like we don't make a difference, yet with our plastic toothpaste cap we are still a part of that. Our responsibility is to say, "Yes, I'm responsible, and I will do what I can to realize that harmony between intention and impact." That is the noble path—closing that gap. That's our work, for at least a lifetime. There is a Jewish saying that goes "It is not your responsibility to finish the task, but neither can you disregard it." That is good to remember so we don't get so overwhelmed that we throw our hands up in the air. It is within our power to take responsibility for the harm we are causing and reduce it. It is within our power to vote, to write that letter, to attend that protest. That's taking responsibility for our place within the body of humanity and the body of the world. This corresponds to the third aspect of right intention, the intention to do no harm. The harm may not be rooted in ill will—who wants to destroy the Pacific Ocean? Rather, this is about cultivating a watchfulness, a sensitivity to where we are causing harm and doing what we can to reduce that.

Reflection

Is there a harm in your life that you have not been addressing, something you know you are doing but haven't shone the full light of awareness on? Is it time to finally take up the cause of addressing it? It could be small, or it could be big. Bring your awareness to it, and make a change.

Tenderness with our responsibility is a place of practice.

BRINGING IT ALL BACK HOME

You may have noticed that the three giants and the three intentions rub noses to some extent. Greed is addressed by the intention of renunciation, hatred by the intention of non–ill will, and delusion by becoming sensitive to when we are causing harm to ourselves and others.

A statement endowed with five factors is well-spoken, not ill-spoken.

It is blameless and unfaulted by knowledgeable people.

Which five?

It is spoken at the right time.

It is spoken in truth.

It is spoken affectionately.

It is spoken beneficially.

It is spoken with a mind of good-will.

—*ANGUTTARA NIKAYA* 5.198

CHAPTER 10

Speech Is a Place of Practice

What we're exploring here is the nobility of words. How do we find and stand up for the nobility of our language, our naming, our storytelling? What we're interested in is speech to set us free, specifically to set us free from suffering. This is a great barometer and lens to look through: How is my speech causing or not causing suffering? How is it liberating? Words don't really encompass anything, nor do names, which is why we have to be careful with them. On the other hand, though, we have to use them, and as I explore below, naming can be a powerful thing despite its limitations. So, the medicine is asking "What's alive now? What's juicy now?" Does this act of speaking, this act of naming, bring healing and nourishment or not?

I love walking down Twenty-Third Street in Manhattan's Chelsea neighborhood, where our Zen center is; it allows me to understand how quickly the mind says, "Oh, I like that person. I don't like that person. That person is cool. That person's not cool." Our brain so often rushes to do that as opposed to being curious about that person and being curious about how we're *not* curious about certain people. It's important to notice the language inside of our head quickly cutting the world into a million parts.

I'm sure that kind of snap judgment was helpful forty thousand years ago, when humans were emerging from the caves and needed to decide what's dangerous and what's not. It's like our cats, Bodhidharma Burrito (remember him?) and Boychik. You can see they're making these quick decisions, avoiding things and going toward others. We are *Homo sapiens*, though, and we have this capacity to actually reflect on that. That's where it's juicy, bringing a curiosity and a self-reflection to the way we fit things into categories in our minds.

Reflection

Try for one day to watch the way you categorize others. How reliable are these judgments? Do they serve your ability to connect to others and learn about them?

Resting on the receptive ground is a place of practice.

RIGHT SPEECH

The Buddha defined right speech as speech that is truthful, not harsh, not divisive, and not disembodied or purposeless. Below, we'll look at these four categories and how they fit into the path

Being Truthful

Before we speak, it's a good practice to ask, "Is this true?" If we want to enhance our practice, we can also ask, "How do I know that it's true?" So much damage is done today by rumors, misinformation, disinformation, and propaganda. We can remove ourselves from this mess to some extent by being careful about what we say or share on social media and having a sense of humility and restraint about it. We can name our sources clearly, and when we don't know something is true on the basis of our own experience, we can be clear about that and say so. One thing I love about the Buddhist path, which I consider part of its nobility, is that it's really about your own freaking experience, not what you heard from someone else.

Lying

The Buddha says that a person should always speak the truth, and in regard to a person who lies without remorse, "there's nothing they're incapable of." This might seem harsh, but there is a real insight in it. A person who lies wants to be right, or doesn't want to be found out. They are holding something very tightly, and who knows what they might do to defend it. It will be difficult for them to walk the path, because this is a path of being truthful, of letting go, of getting real, of opening up.

The Buddha also said about truth that even if you have to deceive someone, for instance to save someone's life, you should still do it without using untrue speech. In other words, you should be aware that you're deceiving the person, but still keep one hand on the truth. There's an old Buddhist story that tells of a time the Buddha was in the forest doing walking meditation, and suddenly somebody ran by looking terrified. The Buddha, who according to legend had great psychic powers, knew what was coming next, so he took one step to the left. A moment later, a bunch of bandits showed up and asked, "While you were standing there, sir, did you see somebody run by?"

And the Buddha said, "No."

This is a great example of keeping your eyes on the truth even while you deceive, like someone out on the sea but still anchored. It's not an excuse to deceive people with true words left and right, of course, but a call to know what you are doing and do it deliberately and carefully while maintaining your care for the truth. This might literally be to protect someone else from harm, but it could also be to protect private information or to avoid harming someone else by sharing a truth that would cause them pain but serve no purpose to share. Numerous psychological studies have shown that people in fact lie a lot and often come to believe their own lies. The practice of always using true words even when you are withholding information is a way of preventing that and of staying wide awake.

Another part of truthfulness that can be hard—very hard—is looking at the shadow of our speech. Even if what we say is true, *why* are we saying it? As William Blake wrote, "A truth told with bad intent beats all the lies you can invent." The fact that something is true is not, ipso facto, a reason to say it or carte blanche to ignore our own motivations or the effects of our speech.

It's always important to reflect on the nobility of our language and whether it is nourishing and helpful or not, even if it's perfectly true. What is my shadow here? Jung said that the shadow is whatever we can't see, and let's face it, that's a lot. I recently heard about a director at a nonprofit who was doing a lot of damage to people around them, using their speech in a Machiavellian way, aiming at consolidating power and controlling other people. Now this person was working for a good cause, and they had great values, but their true speech was motivated by a subtle kind of violence. This ended up overshadowing all the good they were doing.

Reflection

Can you think of a time when you spoke truth with bad intent?

Honesty with kindness is a place of practice.

Harsh Speech

Jean-Paul Sartre said, "Every word has consequences. Every silence, too." One of my students recently came to tell me that they were hurt by my speech, which I appreciated very much. For me, a trusting relationship is built on being able to share our joys and celebrations equally with our hurts, disappointments, and discomforts. They were upset with me because during the recent reckoning with police racism toward Black Americans and violence toward Asian Americans, I had spoken about those things but had never said a word to address the rise in antisemitic violence in recent years. They were especially upset with me because I'm Jewish.

Who we fail to speak up for is also part of our speech. The absence of speaking for people can also be a form of harsh speech, because that absence, that silence, injures and causes suffering. This can also be true for the parts of ourselves we don't speak up for, parts that feel hurt or scared. If you feel into this, you can see that these parts of us are injured by not being spoken out loud. We can get curious about this: "What is my silence about?"

Reflection

Is there something you care about that you're not speaking up for? Is there someone you could help with your speech, but you haven't? Is there a part of yourself that you need to speak out loud?

Not holding back is a place of practice.

When Not to Speak

The real beauty in a relationship is when we can safely come to the other person with ways they've hurt us and be received. Someone dear to me gets so easily triggered by things. They get agitated and can say painful things they don't mean. I've needed to learn to say, "That hurts." I'm learning how to receive harshness and meanness, and not overpersonalize it but also resist it. This person can hear that, and so our relationship remains healthy. Sometimes, though, a person can't hear you when you speak your pain. They are unable to. There's a wonderful book by the Korean poet Ko Un called *Little Pilgrim*, which is based on a famous Indian Buddhist text called *The Flower Garland Sutra*. It tells the story of Sudhana's quest to learn from fifty-two teachers. One teacher is caught in a crevice so deep that nothing can reach them; they can't get out. That is the teaching of this teacher—Sudhana learns how to deal with people who are unreachable.

Sometimes somebody speaks harshly to us, and we would like to be able to respond by arguing, by trying to engage with their better nature, but we need to see when they're caught in the crevice. We need to know when to let go, at least for now—not necessarily forever, but for the time being. We simply need to open up our hands and let go and care for the person equally as well as we care for ourselves.

Divisive Speech

The world is filled with stories that are painful. So many of the stories we tell about other people are really caricatures. We like to think that we can sum someone up with a story, but can we? It's good to bring a healthy dose of skepticism to the stories we tell about others and the stories that we hear.

Divisive speech involves telling a negative story about someone in a way that divides one person from another by harming their opinion of the other person. At times this can cause severe damage or even end relationships or turn friends into enemies. One antidote is curiosity and compassion: to realize that we ourselves suffer from being misunderstood and misrepresented. Are we sure this story we've heard fairly represents the other person, what they actually did, what they actually said, and what it really meant?

The other aspect is being sensitive to our motivations. Why are we telling this negative story or listening to it? Are we doing it because there is a need to warn someone, like telling them about the bad sanitary practices at the restaurant down the street, or the allegations of sexual misconduct against a doctor they are thinking of going to see? Or are we speaking divisively so we can be the one with the dish, to connect, or to make ourselves out as better than the one we're sharing negative stories about?

Disembodied Speech

I like to think of the last kind of harmful speech as disembodied speech. It is speaking with no good purpose, speaking restlessly or neurotically or anxiously because you're filling up a void or you're afraid of silence or what the other person might say.

When we are talking out of fear and anxiety, we are not able to simply be with ourselves and the other people. So the talking doesn't actually aim at connection, it evades it, and it desensitizes us to our own speech. You know, if we're doing it all the time, then we take our speech lightly. We are not in touch with its potential. This undermines the whole project of the nobility of speech.

When we are with another person, we have an opportunity to actually look at them, to take them seriously, to invoke their nobility with our presence and attention. We at the very least have an opportunity for a moment of real human connection. When we turn away, people can feel that. There's no life between us. It reminds me of the habit many of us have of walking past unhoused people on the street, averting our eyes. Homeless people have told me that's more hurtful than not getting spare change. The averted eyes are a form of speech. When we look at someone, really look at them, that's a form of speech.

It can feel more comfortable not to look at them, not to talk to the cashier or the cab driver. We can be so addicted to our comfort that we don't want to risk a little uncomfortable moment and can't even give the dignity of a soft gaze and a "good morning." Instead let's be curious and tender about this discomfort in us; let's breathe through it and then give one another the dignity of our attention. That speaks louder than words.

Reflection

As you go about your day, try committing to looking fully at (but not ogling!) the people you come into contact with. If something arises naturally that you'd like to say, try saying it. You may be surprised how many connections you make, and how good it feels, perhaps!

Connection is a place of practice.

THE TRUTH OF THIS MOMENT

Shunryu Suzuki, one of the first Japanese Soto Zen teachers in America, said, "If we treat every moment as your last, it's not a preparation for something else." The application for this thought goes beyond being in the present moment. We can bring it to thought, words, and actions. Can we untangle our tongues and learn how to use our speech in this way? Can we say what's true right now in this moment, what is vital and connected and true, and not part of a strategy? Can we remember that what we say seems true to us right now, but may not be the final truth or the truth of the next moment when we've learned more than we know now? I have gotten into the practice of adding "until now" or "up until this point" to my sentences when speaking about myself or other people. What I'm saying has been true up until now; yet right now, what else is possible?

I had a conversation with someone recently who said, "I'm a fearful person. I'm difficult. Things don't work out for me." We create these narratives and *abracadabra*—they become sentences of power. The word *abracadabra* is an old Aramaic phrase, *abara* meaning "may it be created," and *cadabra* meaning "I have spoken." So the way we speak about ourselves, the way we name ourselves, can become a self-fulfilling prophecy. Speech has that power. When we say, "I'm this way" or "I'm that way," we're defining ourselves, and when we define ourselves as being this way or that way, we always make ourselves smaller. The truth is that we're too complex to define, and we can't get a bird's-eye view of ourselves that would allow for accurate definitions anyway. What if that person played around with saying, "I'm a brave person. I'm easy to be around. Things work out for me"? Could they see how that could just as easily be "true"? We're all making up stories about ourselves, so we may as well play around with making up new nourishing ones. What would happen if we tried that? This can be a good road to leaving behind the effects of our toxic speech about ourselves and others.

Reflection

Can you think of three or four ways you habitually define yourself? Do they really tell the whole story?

Imagining the expansive story is a place of practice.

LIVING WORDS

Instead of telling ourselves these self-fulfilling, self-limiting cement-and-concrete stories, we can speak what the Zen tradition calls "living words." In the history of Zen, we have placed a high value on living, spontaneous, intelligent words that can "give life or take it away," which is another way of saying that they can nourish or, when needed, cut through dead weight that it would be better to let go of.

This is the type of speech that we find in koans, or the records of the dialogues of past masters, and also how we speak in Zen mondo, or combat, when Zen practitioners challenge one another's understanding in spontaneous dialogue. It is the type of speech that evokes the feeling of a person who is connected to what they're saying in the right now; they're embodied, vital, attuned to what is happening, and speaking their truth. Even if they are wrong, it's still nourishing for others. They are not absorbed into manipulation or repeating "the story," by which I mean stale thoughts, stale narratives, or words that are aiming at getting cookies or massaging their own anxieties.

When we stay grounded in our bodies, breathing from the belly, we can practice speaking honestly and compassionately like this.

Names

The word *narrative* comes from the Latin root *narrare*, which means "to tell a tale," but when I hear it I think *narrow*. We have to be careful about how narrow our narratives can be. That said, what we name people and things is important. Most spiritual traditions have naming ceremonies, which reflects this importance. Some names are nourishing, and some are not.

I love naming. It's a big thing, for good and for ill. The danger of naming is when we box ourselves in, identifying ourselves as one way or another. In earlier chapters, I shared that I had a clear identity as a victim when I was younger. Terrible things happened to me, yes, but I realized it's such a small view of who I am, just one slice of my life. I had experienced sexual and physical abuse, and antisemitic attacks on my body. I'd experienced all those things, but what is also true is that I've had so many moments in my life of absolute amazement: getting down on the ground and staring at the intricate beauty of moss; swimming with sea turtles in Mexico; jumping off a cliff in Jamaica and experiencing the terror and the exhilaration of hitting the water.

I've had different names at different points of my life. My parents named me Daniel, after my father's best friend. I didn't know who this person was, but I did know that my dad and mom had loved and cared for him. Still, the name never resonated with me, especially after I understood that its Hebrew meaning was "the judgment of God"!

Many years later I was given my first Buddhist name, Ansho. The character for *an* means peace and *sho* means true, so it means "true peace." The name given is what the teacher imagines you growing into. When I was given that name, I thought, *Wow, that seems really far away,* and it felt kind of impossible. But the point of the name was not to look at it from the point of view of who I had been and what I thought my limits were. So I chose to take that name on, and it became a way of experiencing myself differently. Many years later, I was ordained as a monk and was given the name Koshin, which means *boundless heart.* I legally changed my name, because that felt important. It feels to me like the name is my vow. In Zen, a vow is important; you could say that all of our practice is rooted in our vow to wake up to the reality of our lives for our own sakes and the sakes of others. Yet we also have a personal sense of vow that is not fully communicable to others. My name, Koshin, expresses that personal sense of vow for me.

Now, on the rare occasion someone calls me Daniel, it feels strange, because I identify as Koshin. Am I only Koshin, though, or still Daniel? While I was in a poetry class in Provincetown, Massachusetts, at the Fine Arts Work Center, the fabulous poet Olga Broumas was going around and asking, "What's your name, and what's the meaning of your name?" I said, "Well, I have three names that I've been given. One means 'God's judgment,' one is 'true peace,' and one means 'boundless heart.' So you see, they are quite different."

She said, "Not to me." That made me think about the shadow side of names, which is the way we use them to deny aspects of ourselves or to separate things. You know, *I'm not judgmental, I'm not God's judgment, I'm not this*, or *I'm not that*. So another part of language and right speech to me is also watching when we say we are *not* something. For instance, as a spiritual person, I see myself as not being a fundamentalist, but is that the whole story? If I think so, I haven't looked deeply into myself and found the place where I am a fundamentalist. How can I not be anything that exists in this world?

Reflection

What are you in the habit of saying you're not? Is that the whole truth? Is there a way in which you are that which you reject?

Resting in possibilities is a place of practice.

What we plant in the soil of contemplation, we shall reap in the harvest of action.

—MEISTER ECKHART

When we face pain in relationships our first response is often to sever bonds rather than to maintain commitment.

—BELL HOOKS

CHAPTER 11

Action Is a Place of Practice

Earlier, I referenced the saying "the road to hell is paved with good intentions." This happens when we believe we have good intentions, but we don't attend to what we are actually doing. We are wrapped up in the idea of what we're doing versus what we are actually doing. Yet our *actions* are our true belongings, not our *beliefs* about the way we act. They are a clear indicator of whether we are walking the walk and not just talking the talk. The way to wake up to this is to attend to the impact of our actions, which can often set off a needed alarm bell.

My friend Marie was in the grocery store, and another shopper would not move their grocery cart even a little to let her get by. If you asked Marie if she was a caring and generous person, likely she would say yes. In the cart incident, she's "defending her space" or "standing up for her rights." That's the false patina of good intentions we paint over the way we're acting.

Years ago I met Peter Malkin, the Israeli secret agent who caught Adolf Eichmann, the Nazi mass murderer, in Argentina. The thing was, in the weeks leading up to the capture of Eichmann, Malkin had to watch him going about his daily life. There was the monster buying groceries, the monster hugging his kids, the monster kissing his wife or going for a peaceful evening walk. Did the monster know he was a monster? Apparently not, because if he did, how could he do any of these things? After they captured Eichmann, Malkin got to know him and they discussed his life. Eichmann did not view himself as monstrous; he believed he had been engaged in a worthy project and had done the right thing. Clearly we humans have to be careful about having faith in our own good intentions. The way to untangle our actions is to pay attention to what we're doing and what its actual impacts are. This is the next aspect of the Eightfold Path we'll explore. The fact is, life is giving us feedback about our actions all the time, and if we tune in to that, it's an incomparable way of beginning to untangle our actions and our lives.

Reflection

Is there a place in your life where you believe you have good intentions, but the impact of your behavior doesn't match them? Could there be something missing in your understanding of your own intentions?

Investigation is a place of practice.

FEEDBACK

There is so much power in becoming truly receptive to the feedback the world is giving us about our actions. This includes feedback from our own body. If I'm feeling tight in my chest when someone is sharing something with me, it's an indication that I'm being defensive. Staying soft in our bellies can be a way of staying curious and open. It's tempting to take a stand on our beliefs about what we're doing and shut out the feedback we get from life. We may have strong beliefs that a certain type of behavior is right, or that we are acting with integrity, but we're not paying attention to how our action is actually affecting others. Truth be told, this happens all the time, and it's easier to see with other people. Yet it's equally true about ourselves. We're not immune to the types of foolishness and blindness we see in others. In order for our actions to bear the fruit that we want, we need to get in touch with what our own bodies, other people, and life in general are telling us. We have to be sensitive to impact, which means that we have to be able to be receptive to feedback.

Years ago we did an organizational review at the Zen center. We had an outside consultant come in and interview twenty-eight people around the organization and make some recommendations. It was humbling, and to get feedback about myself, to see and hear my impact, was interesting. There are moments when I don't listen so well, and there are moments when I'm not so skillful and not so helpful, to put it mildly. It was kind of like lifting the curtain and seeing what's behind. It felt refreshing and balancing to me (and not surprising) to experience the whole range of impacts that I am responsible for.

I imagine some people were upset about what was said about them and perhaps felt victimized by it. This can be a symptom of being invested in the idea of our good intentions and opposed to untangling our actions. If we're able to stay in the body and to breathe, we can be receptive to that kind of feedback coming back.

On the other hand, if we're receptive to the feedback that's coming back to us all the time, then at times that we do get direct or explicit feedback, it's often not so shocking because we're already in touch with our patterns. There are fewer surprises.

Refining our actions is also about the work that each of us has to do so that we can create a space where people feel comfortable giving us feedback. It takes all parties in a relationship to be open to that. It's about actively creating a self that encourages feedback from other people. This is all in the way that you conduct yourself: Do you ask others for their opinions? Do you receive criticism graciously? Do you acknowledge and welcome the truths of others?

SIX REFLECTIONS

The Buddha offered six training guidelines whose aim was to free us from types of remorse and interpersonal chaos that derail our practice, our lives, and other people's lives as well. One we already covered: speech. The other five are killing, lying, stealing, sexuality, and intoxication. In the Zen tradition, these areas of reflection have been understood not just literally but also psychologically. Let's explore them together.

KILLING

The Buddha taught that we should not intentionally take life. Yet even if we are careful not to deliberately take the life of any living creatures, our actions are still tangled up with killing and taking away life. We all know that on some level. This is true in obvious ways, like when we unknowingly step on an ant, buy goods that come from a sweatshop, eat meat, or even eat an innocent broccoli floret. It's also true on subtler levels, though, in the way we interact with people and the way we treat ourselves. How do we really look at this?

When I walk into a room, I'm aware that I tend to be an extrovert. I can have a lot of energy and take up a lot of space. So when I walk into a room, I have to be very aware of how that might impact other people and how most people I know are not extroverted, and especially people who are drawn into shyness, which tends to attract more introverted folks. And so if I come in with too much energy, it can kill people's ability to connect. I've gotten lots of feedback about being so "big" and learning how to modulate—at least for a lifetime.

The nobility here is knowing that my actions can harm in all kinds of subtle and not so subtle ways, like when we're not paying attention to our effect on people and we kill the connection. We can be caught in thinking, *Well, this is the way I am*, and not being willing to be sensitive and adjust. To me it's actually also much more interesting and engaging to pay attention and modulate. My teacher James Hillman loved the word *interesting*, which comes from the Latin word *interesse*. That word breaks down into *inter* and *esse*, or "being between." He liked to say that we should take an interest in the between, in what exists between people, in that dynamic space. Good medicine.

This means you're not just expressing yourself, but you're watching, interested in the impact, and you're willing to modify how you're acting. Meditation practice is important in this regard, because it helps you learn how to build this dynamic fulcrum in yourself. When we're in the realm of thinking, we can become reactive, rigid, or disattuned, but when we're in the body, we can stay more pliant, more sensitive, and more grounded in the reality of what's actually happening in the present. To be between is actually to be in a relationship where I matter and you matter.

Reflection

Is there a relationship in which you could attend to the in between? Try, the next time you're with that person, to shift your attention away from yourself, or from your ideas about them, and instead to attend to the space in between. Try to keep that space alive and dynamic, and see what happens.

Allowing the in between is a place of practice.

Eating

Throughout the world, when people talk about killing, what comes up at some point is the ethics of food: Are you a carnivore or a vegetarian or a vegan? For most of us, food is the sphere in which we most obviously make choices about violence. A fruitful way to approach this issue, rather than having a hard and fast rule about it, is to be in relationship with the food you're eating and with the beings who produce it and the beings you are eating. Some kind of ethical stance will come from that, but the objective is not to have a dead relationship to the food. You're not killing that relationship between you and what's sustaining you.

We can get righteous about this, though, as I'm sure you know.

I used to be righteous in that way, as a militant vegan. I was one of those people you didn't want to have dinner with, because I would be judgmental and up on my soapbox. Maybe I was alive to my relationship to animals, and yet I was killing the relationship between myself and the others at the table.

Something shifted for me when I was in Mexico eating dinner at the home of a local poet, and they put this food down and—let's just say it wasn't rice and beans. I was about to say, *No, I don't eat this kind of food, I'm a vegan.* But suddenly, looking at the effort they had put into presenting the food beautifully, the spirit with which they were sharing it, and the loving dynamic building between the people, I realized that in judging them, I was, in a subtle way, a killer. I'm not saying people should not be vegan. The problem was not in eating or not waiting for the food, but in the way I related to them. At that moment, feeling holier than them, I was about to kill something alive for the sake of animals that were already dead.

Suddenly I realized my own hypocrisy, and that was being, and having been for years, a vegan killer. Avoiding aiding and abetting suffering with one's food choices is good—and again, I'm not criticizing the attempt to do that—but my own sense of self-righteousness was excessive. Aren't plants living beings too, after all? And the insects that die in food preparation? There are virtues in not taking part in the modern agribusiness industry, with its brutality toward animals and its huge climate footprint, but in my own small way I was still a killer. The truth is that we are connected to the whole catastrophe, and our hands are never clean. We can't stand in judgment over the rest of humanity.

Sometimes when I'm teaching, I invite people to explore this question, to ask, "How am I a killer?" If we are honest about this, then we can take responsibility for it and make decisions to reduce the killing that we are doing, causing, encouraging, or rewarding. That's one way of expressing compassion for all of the killed out there. Yet we will also stay in touch with the sense of humility we should have about this, and the compassion we should have for all of our fellow killers.

LYING: GETTING IN TOUCH WITH AND SPEAKING THE TRUTH

To me, lying is intimately connected with vulnerability. I believe that when we lie, it's because we're afraid of exposing something about ourselves.

"I think the greatest illusion we have," the activist and playwright V writes, "is that denial protects us." She continues, "It's a weird thing about truth; it actually protects you. What really makes you vulnerable is when you're lying, because you know you're going to get caught, even by your own mind. That you know you're a liar." When you do finally tell the truth, there's a strange relief that comes with it.

One of my students told me a story once about a man she was assisting in his dying process. His final wish was to see his daughter, from whom he was estranged. My student had to put a lot of effort into finding the daughter, because the man wasn't in touch with her at all. When she did find her and related her father's dying wish, the daughter said, "I don't want to see him. I hate him, and I'm glad he's dying."

My student went back to the man and told him that his daughter wouldn't come. He pleaded with her to try again. So she went back to the daughter, and this time the daughter acquiesced. "Okay," she said. "I'm not going to stay long, but I'll come." My student joyfully brought the news back to the father. She was so happy that she was able to aid with such a beautiful reconciliation.

The day the daughter arrived at the hospital, my student was standing outside the door in anticipation. She saw the daughter fly into the room. As soon as she got in, my student heard her say to her father, "You're one of the most awful people I've ever known. You've caused more harm to me than anyone I've ever met. I hate your guts." And then she turned on her heel and left.

My student went into the room in a panic, apologizing. "I'm so sorry," she said to the father. "I didn't know that was going to happen." The father responded, "That's exactly what I wanted to happen. The truth is, I *was* a terrible father. She's never had the opportunity to tell me that to my face, and I know it was eating her alive." So that was his last gift to his daughter—the gift of having her truth heard, which was perhaps a relief to them both.

There are the garden-variety lies we tell (I remember when I was teaching poetry, I had a student who had three grandmothers die), but another way to think about lying is as our unwillingness to examine what is really true.

For me the most challenging lies between people are lies of omission: what we don't say.

In Japanese culture there is a word, *ma*, that describes the space between things. It is what makes Japanese art, architecture, and gardens so unique. So much attention is brought to the gap, to the pause, that you can really see the stone, the scroll, the tree, the shape of a branch. Without attention to the space between, there is no true beauty and life. This is what happens in many relationships.

As stories throughout time tell, when people can't adapt to change and talk about it together, the relationship breaks: Baba Yaga and the adventurers, Chiron and Hercules, Pharaoh and Moses, Darth Vader and Obi Wan Kenobi, and on and on. The lie of omission created in relationships causes confusion and distrust, the relationships suffer, and perhaps the once deeply held respect for each other is shattered, the bond broken.

My teacher, Sensei Dorothy Dai En Friedman, says, "It takes everything to be free." We have to be willing to truly be in the layers and discomfort together. With shared commitment, it is possible, and preciously rare. Both people need to be fully willing to get into the muck and learn how to be in it together. When this is possible, my experience is that deeper intimacy and trust arise.

The Zen Peacemakers understand not-lying as listening and speaking from the heart. It's a prompt to stay connected to what is authentic for you, to ask yourself what you conceal about your own life and to be brave in hearing the answer. We all have those weird little pockets of concealment that we create, don't we? I've never met someone without them, anyway.

One person who exemplified the refusal to lie to himself was the historical Buddha, which is partly what makes his story so inspiring. I'm sure you know people who went into certain careers because their parents wanted them to—"I'm a lawyer because my mom was a lawyer," and so on and so forth. The Buddha's dad was like that, too. He wanted his son to be a clan leader, kind of like a king, like himself, instead of what the Buddha might want to be. When the Buddha was born, his fortune was told. The oracles said that he would be either a great king, like his father, or a great spiritual leader. Well, his dad sure knew which one of those options he preferred.

He took great pains to make sure that his son was always distracted by some luxury or another and didn't let him leave the walls of the palace, so he couldn't follow a spiritual path.

Eventually the Buddha did leave the palace, and what he saw—essentially suffering, frailty, sickness, and death—struck him to the core. It was the Buddha's "oh shit" moment. He could have gone back to the palace and lived out the rest of his days in pleasure, but he couldn't ignore the truth of what was in front of him. So, he walked away.

In our lives, there are often expectations put upon us by another, whether it be our parents, society, what we read in magazines, or whatever. These expectations are almost like an overlay: what our life is "supposed" to be. They have less to do with us (or reality) than with some vague external idea. And then we go about measuring ourselves against that idea. That's why what happened with the Buddha is so interesting; he encountered something within himself that felt at odds with his overlay—and used that incongruency to pivot.

To learn how to be who we are, it's essential to actually listen to what's true instead of what we've been told is true. From this space, we can practice speaking what is actually true from our lived experience. This is the practice of not-lying.

Reflection

What do you conceal about your life? How can you see and act in accordance with your deepest values?

How can you be wholehearted and brave in your relationships?

Transparency is a place of practice.

STEALING

From a literal standpoint, stealing is taking stuff that's not yours. On a subtler level, though, we can be aware of how we take space from others in our conversations and psychically. This might be on the level of privilege: Are there some rooms we walk into where people give us more space because we are perceived as the same gender, sexuality, class, race, and ethnicity, and we just take what's offered to us?

On the other hand, not sharing yourself can also be a form of stealing. It's not allowing people to get to know you. I know my pain comes from not being a full person with others. In the Jewish tradition this is called a gonif das, a thief of knowledge. When you are not honest with others, when you don't disclose yourself, you are denying them that little piece of reality that is you, and you may also be breaking the proper feedback loop between them and the universe. In that sense you are stealing from them. This kind of stealing often comes from a feeling of deficiency, which drives us to hide what we actually are or not even show up at all. So the fact of learning how to not steal is actually learning that you have enough.

When we feel that the way we are is unacceptable to others or to ourselves, we end up stealing from our multiplicity. If I'm not seeing and accepting all the different parts of myself, chances are I'm going to steal from you too. I'm not going to allow you your capacity to be your full self either. So stealing comes from a poverty mentality of feeling like you don't have enough, yet ironically it also impoverishes.

Generosity is an antidote to stealing, both on the literal level and also on the level we're exploring here, because it can be generous to share your true self with other people.

Reflection

Who do you not disclose your real self to? Is it possible you are stealing something important from them?

Openness is a place of practice.

SEXUALITY

The internet is primarily used for porn. That's staggering, isn't it? People are looking for pleasure or release or connection, and our sexual selves are so important to us. I'm not making a pronouncement about pornography here, but what we do know from watching porn is that it doesn't really work as a source of those things in a sustained way. Yet sexual pleasure, release, and connection are fundamental concerns for *Homo sapiens* and important parts of life. Knowing this, how do we function in the world where we can treat other beings sexually, including ourselves, with respect and dignity?

We often don't think about how when we're having sex with one person, it affects communities and broader relationships. We're not an island. We are not alone in the world, even though we may feel alone. I know many people who have become hungry ghosts looking for the next great sexual experience. I have zero interest in whether people have one partner or many partners; that's not my point. What we can be interested in is how we can have relationships that actually have the nobility of true pleasure.

Reflection

Does our relationship to sex reflect the dignity of our sexuality and that of others?

Tenderness is a place of practice.

Sexual Misconduct

The oldest guide to sexual misconduct in the Buddhist community focuses on consent and community. There is no discussion of sexual preferences or marital status, just these basic categories. They say that you should not sleep with someone who can't consent to it, or whose commitments to other people or a community would be broken. This reflects the fact that in some cases a person can't meaningfully consent—like when power dynamics or force is involved, or when one person is a minor. In other cases, even if one person does consent, their partner or their community can't, as in the case of having sex with a celibate cleric. On the other hand, if someone is in a polyamorous relationship, or they are not a religious celibate, then no one's commitments are broken by having sex with you.

Reflection

Have you been impacted by this issue of sex without consent or respect for community, whether that is a large community or a community of two? Have you impacted others? How has that affected the way you express your value of non-harming?

Encountering all beings with respect and dignity is a place of practice.

Tricky

What makes sex so tricky is that we often don't know how to talk about it. We're not coming from a place of honesty and acceptance that we are sexual beings, and that we all have this common sexual life. If 70 to 80 percent of people use porn, like the data suggests, then why is it that being publicly outed as a porn user would be mortifying for most people and maybe even cost them their relationships or career? That's a big lie, a big disconnect. I'm not just talking about porn here, but about the reality of our lives as sexual beings. Is there any other area where there is so much subterfuge and shame about something so universal as our sexuality?

So considering that, how do we get into a positive relationship with sexuality, and really live in between us, *inter-esse*? I want to live a wholehearted life, which is an honest life. And I also have sexual desire. How do we nurture and nourish that in a way that treats ourselves and others with respect and dignity?

In a story I love, a nun is propositioned by a monk, who sends her a note that says something like, "After the sermon tonight, meet me out back." So right before the sermon begins, she stands up in front of everyone and addresses him, and says, "If you desire me so much, embrace me here and now." This story is clever on many levels, including the obvious one that she safely ends the monk's secret pursuit of her, upholds her own integrity before the community, and challenges him.

There's another level that I think is worth looking at. By inviting him before the community, she puts his action back into its proper context. His advance does not concern only the two of them, and certainly it does not concern only his desire. His pursuit of her concerns the entire community that they are both responsible to. When she says, "If you desire me so much, embrace me here and now" she is saying, "If you think your come-on to me is right and good, then do it here where the whole community it affects can join you in deciding about that." The parallel for this story in terms of someone in a monogamous relationship would be to invite the person hitting on you to do it in front of your partner. Really, of course, there are no secrets. When we do something that affects a whole community, but in secret, thinking no one will know, we are fooling ourselves.

When It's Right

The first time I saw Chodo, I felt a desire in a way that I hadn't ever felt before. It was not just sexual desire; it was that I knew when this person walked in the room my whole life was going to change. We were in a Zen practice center, and I got more than a little distracted during the walking meditation as a result! I found myself peeking at him and being really, really smiley. The thing was, I had a partner, who was there and who I was committed to. Yet I remember this incredible feeling that my life was going to change and that my relationship had to change—that, in fact, it was over.

I knew the relationship I was in would have to end before anything could happen with Chodo, and ironically, I didn't see Chodo again for six years. I so loved the person I was with, but a romantic relationship was not the right loving form. Sometimes it's learning to appreciate that relationships—sexual relationships and friendships too—need to change form, which can happen when we stay curious about whether the form is really attuned for both people. Sometimes it's not what it was or what we had hoped it would be, and we need to change the form of our commitment to each other rather than break it.

INTOXICATION

An intoxicant is anything that harms our clarity, dilutes the mind, or deludes us about our actions. These days distraction is a major intoxicant. We have a challenge with just being with ourselves. We are hooked into the stimulation of our devices, or we are keeping ourselves busy. We're always one step ahead of the crest of our feelings, running from ourselves.

How are we turning on the fog machine in our lives to hide the details from ourselves? With all this fog pouring out, we don't clearly see the impact of our actions. People often tell me, "I'm not good at paying attention." We have to be careful not to use the kinds of stories that further our hypnosis. All of us have a gazillion thoughts a moment. When we're being pulled out of the reality of the present moment, that's a time to get curious. It's a time to be humble and curious, like, *Wow, what is that about? What's my deal here?*

I have a wonderful friend, a Buddhist practitioner whose house I use to spend lots of weekends at. What I found puzzling were the shifts in behavior from bright and cheerful to snappy and depressed as the day went on, and then they would usually just pass out. This person believed in clarity and connections, but their actions were not clear, not in tune. I asked Chodo, "What's the deal here?"

"They're an alcoholic," Chodo said. It was clear to me immediately: That was the answer.

This person was totally wonderful and yet struggled with an addiction to alcohol and suffered with it. It alienated them from a lot of people. Yet all of us have these gaps between our values and our actions, and often the bridge that carries us away from ourselves is intoxication. This is literally true of alcohol and other intoxicants, but on a subtler level our internal fog machines can alienate us from others at least as much.

This inquiry into intoxication, we should know, never ends. It's a steady inquiry into what causes my fingers to flip the switch of the fog machine. For me that doesn't mean that you drink or you don't, but the question is, are you taking steps to reduce the intoxication that cloud aspects of your life you don't want to deal with?

Reflection

What do you intoxicate yourself with, and when? The next time you have an urge to self-medicate in that way, can you sit with your feelings and see if it passes? Gentle steps like this can ease us into more continuous sobriety. Clarity is a place of practice.

In the mundane, nothing is sacred. In sacredness, nothing is mundane.

—EIHEI DOGEN ZENJI

CHAPTER 12

Work Is a Place of Practice

One-third of our lives is spent at work. This is a depressing statistic for many, who may find their job to be meaningless, degrading, or just plain boring. There's plenty of advice to be had from "influencers" whose main skill seems to lie in inspiring other people to try to be "influencers" as well. They will tell you to quit your day job, cook up half a dozen lucrative side hustles, or use their fail-safe method for relocating to an "inexpensive" country and outsourcing all your pesky work tasks so you can work a handful of hours a week and windsurf the rest. Perhaps this is a fabulous life for some. For most, though, none of those things are possible. Some can't just shift jobs; they have debts and bills and people relying on them.

No matter what our situation, we need to find meaning in the job we have.

MEANINGFUL WORK

It's impossible to meaningfully think about livelihood until we are pretty in touch with who we are as a human being. We go into the externalizing first, like "I gotta get a job." In American culture you could argue at this point that there isn't much training in unfolding who you are, and so for many of us we discover this through the jobs we try.

In high school I worked briefly at the Gap. I learned how to fold T-shirts, which I still am very good at to this day, but at the time I didn't want to spend my days doing that, and I was privileged enough that I could make another choice. Eventually I found that I enjoyed jobs where I could see directly that I was bringing joy to other people, whether that was as a waiter or a camp counselor. So I was beginning to discover along the way who I was, and what jobs would reflect that and be nourishing, both to myself and to others.

Along with this lack of encouragement in deep self-discovery before we enter the work world, once we do, we are also not often taught to consider how we actually function in our work lives. Once we are in the working world and are actively getting a job, choosing jobs, leaving jobs, going to another job, adding another job, adding a side hustle, and deciding how many passive income streams to try to add on, the question is, what motivates us? As we move through the seasons of our lives, meaning becomes more important. What are our values? What are our beliefs? What are our intentions? How do we want to be in the time of our one precious life?

Cleaning the Toilet

It is also important to realize that whatever job we find ourselves needing to do has value. A few years into my Zen training I found myself working at a macrobiotic vegan Mexican restaurant, and it was a great training in service to others. Many of the customers were, you could say, very particular about their food, and meeting their needs required patience, compassion, and attention to detail. "Is this water triple-filtered? Where exactly do these beans come from?"

Meanwhile, in Zen retreats I was also learning about service, and these two things fused in my mind. When you're serving the community their meals, you enter the dining room bowing on your knees and serve each person in their three bowls. The Zen ritual teaches you so much about the dignity and beauty of giving food to others, and that can influence how you feel about it in other so-called mundane settings.

I never had appreciated serving so much before, and learning how to do that was so amazing, to learn how to appreciate what I so rarely appreciated. In Zen training work is spiritual practice, and training in that is called samu. For me as a young person it was life changing to learn that work tasks, even those seemingly mundane and boring work, were considered sacred practice in Zen. In retrospect, folding T-shirts doesn't look meaningless to me. It can be done beautifully in a spirit of service, like most things.

It's important to know deep in our bones that there is not a moment in our life that we can't practice. When I was training to be what's called a "senior student," the value of that role, contrary to what some might think, was that you did the most menial and necessary work! So you're actually in charge of cleaning all the toilets, for instance, for all the monks and participants, and that's thought to be really special training. Cleaning collective pissy and shitty toilets helps us to learn to appreciate that there is no menial job.

Dogen wrote a beautiful essay about this that has been

important in our tradition called *Instructions to the Cook*. The great twentieth-century teacher Kosho Uchiyama wrote a commentary on it called *How to Cook Your Life*, in which he tells this story of the monastery cook at a monastery in the Wutai Mountains, which are sacred to Manjushri, the bodhisattva of cutting through our delusions. While the cook was stirring the rice, the Bodhisattva Manjushri himself suddenly appeared above the pot, and the cook whapped him with a cooking spoon. Later the cook said, "Even if the Buddha were to appear above the pot, I would whap him, too!"

Visions and dreams are wonderful if we're still embodying our life, if we're still stirring the rice when the rice needs to be stirred. Even daydreaming about something exalted like a bodhisattva is still daydreaming and can keep us from the here and now of being wholly present to the task at hand. The reality is what is sacred.

WHAT KEEPS US FROM THE POTENTIAL OF OUR WORK?

One doctor I've worked with had gotten caught up in the idea of being a doctor. She realized, during her training with us, that she had stopped looking her patients in the eye. In fact, she had stopped making eye contact with her patients when she was in residency. She had to tell these two parents that their baby had died in the womb, and she did not know how to do that. She was a deeply caring person, a deeply loving person, but she got so uncomfortable, and then she came to cling to this story of discomfort. It was through learning how to be with her fear and discomfort, staying in relationship with those things, and asking for help that transformation came.

Slowly she learned that she could actually be with her feelings, and through that be with other people no matter what she needed to say to them. She could create spaces, which we co-created together, and she was able to actually begin looking at her patients again. And she began loving them again and feeling sorrow with them and feeling the mystery of it again. This process took time and support. It was amazing to see her start showing up to our work together with this super energized feeling. I was amazed because when she came the first day I was thinking, *Well, she's in trouble.* Her shoulders were hunched, and her head was kind of down. She was almost collapsed into herself. Over the months of our work together in contemplative medicine, she started to engage, her shoulders went down, and her head went up. She was looking people in the eye, and she had so much energy. It was like a weighted blanket had come off her and she remembered who she was. "I've been almost like Rip Van Winkle," she said. "I have been asleep for a long time."

Difficult emotions can come up in our work: fear, hopelessness, anger, greed, pride. There is a danger in accepting that as simply part of our work life and cutting it off from our full humanity. We might not be that way at home, but at work we just shut down and accept it. Feeling we're alone, though, is not the same thing as actually being alone. If we find ourselves in that situation, we can reach out to others who are struggling with the same thing.

Our work can become a mirror, and when it does, it reflects our practice back to us. There really isn't any dead time in our lives, you know. Heaven forbid. No moment will repeat itself. Every moment can be the practice of waking up to our lives.

Reflection

Is there a state of mind or a behavior that you suffer in your work life that you'd never suffer elsewhere?

Engagement is a place of practice.

WRONG LIVELIHOOD?

When I lived on a kibbutz, which is a kind of Israeli agricultural commune, I was briefly assigned to work in the plastic factory. What made me quit was not that it was boring—though to me it was—but rather that there was no ventilation. That's an important thing—air. I felt grateful that I had the privilege to change. I also thought of the perhaps millions of people who are working in factories with no ventilation making us things we use every day. I felt heartbroken for these people I imagined in factories around the globe. They transferred me to the avocado groves. I loved picking avocados, thankfully, and there was air aplenty.

There are some types of work that are hard but give you a feeling of connection to the work, like (for me) avocado picking, and then there are other forms of work that might be difficult but can still be made into practice because of how they're approached. But then there are other kinds of work that are actually harmful to you, like working in a plastic factory.

It's important to ask if our work is doing harm, either to ourselves or others. As we explored in the last chapter, that's something we can feel in our bodies and our minds. It could be that working as a receptionist is harming me; maybe the boss is toxic or the work doesn't suit me. Maybe being visionary and doing creative work sings for me, and administrative stuff is such a chore that it drains my life—or the opposite, I love the work of ordering and problem solving that makes for a good administrator, and I'm happy to leave the visioning to others.

Untangling our intentions on this path means being non-harming and non-exploitative, and for our actions and values to be in line. As a natural extension of this, we become sensitized to how we can reduce harm in our work life, which might mean switching jobs. It might not be possible, though, to do that, at least not for some time. That may be so, but there is still scope for meeting a job we can't escape in a new way. We can have an idealization about what job we'd like to have, and yet what can we do to bring some goodness to where we are right now? To me the practice of livelihood is taking responsibility for our work life in full. It's as simple as that.

BELONGING

When we can't find a sense of belonging at work, we may need to search for it elsewhere. This can be incredibly important for our mental health. This was always the case, and the COVID-19 pandemic only underscored it. I have had the experience of working with many different kinds of people—from acrobats, actors, rabbis, hedge fund managers, factory workers, porters, and parents to bankers—and when they are not satisfied there, they find balance in a community of shared values and putting a stake down there. I've found that people who are willing to put down roots in a community have more capacity to deal with difficulty because they feel more supported.

Reflection

Is there a community where you feel a sense of belonging, or where you think you might feel that way? Often the way into community is simply to show up and see what you can offer, which might be as simple as schlepping chairs. If there is a community you've been thinking of joining but haven't, why not show up once a week for a month and see what happens?

Belonging is a place of practice.

WILLING TO FAIL

My oldest friend, Todd, did martial arts training in Japan. For the first six months, he spent all day being thrown and learning how to fall. There were broken bones; there was blood; people got sent to the hospital. The teacher's message, to riff on teaching from Sensei White, was *You'll never be free until you learn to fall without fear.* How powerful we could be if we all learned to fall! Life will teach us this anyway—or at least try to—so we might as well embrace it.

Among my students, I can also see the opposite of this. I see an intense fear of public and personal failure, of not doing the correct thing. This fear can be paralyzing, and the only cure for it is to do the wrong thing publicly over and over again and survive anyway. Part of being an adult in our work is being willing to experience nondefensive embarrassment.

Reflection

Is there something you've been wanting to do at work but are afraid to try for fear of failure? Is it safe enough to try? Safe enough to fail?

Falling down is a place of practice.

EVERYTHING MATTERS

Everything matters, and that includes our livelihood. I'm not saying this to guilt you or to show you what a fuck-up you are. I mean to express that everything matters because everything is an opportunity. Moving every dish, every bowl, every grain of rice is an opportunity to see how we're functioning in our work and how to wake up into nobility. This doesn't mean that we're going to become serene Buddhas in the workplace or perfect masters of economic and interpersonal jiu-jitsu; it means that we'll make the changes we need to bring our livelihoods into line with our values, and what we can't change we will accept so that we can focus on expressing our values wherever possible.

Reflection

Is there one thing in your work that you can change into nourishment? Something small to start?

Right livelihood is a place of practice.

You are too serious, Orlando. And yet, not serious enough.

—VIRGINIA WOOLF

CHAPTER 13

Effort Is a Place of Practice

One of the Buddha's most beautiful metaphors compares the way we approach our effort to the way a musician tunes their lute. If it is too slack, there is no harmony; if it is too tight, the strings snap. Always one to tailor his metaphors to his audience, this example was given by the Buddha to Sona, a monk who had been a lutist before he became a monk. When I heard this, it inspired me to realize that I was both too loose and too tight in some ways. Have you ever felt that way?

SIT FOR THIRTY YEARS

Maezumi Roshi was once talking to a student, and Roshi began crying. The student said, "What's happening?"

Maezumi Roshi said, "Oh, it's just so painful that so few people stay with their training."

For many years my practice was such that I was "kind of practicing." I would give myself entirely to the practice only when I felt the conditions were right. When there wasn't a movie I wanted to go see, or there weren't friends to go out with, and I had exhausted all other forms of distraction, then the conditions were right! Many of us have this habit. We don't have to be a Zen person to appreciate this. How many of us don't fully live our lives? We wait, we wait, we wait. We're waiting for conditions to be "right." Yet what if it is practice itself that makes the conditions right?

Finally, I began to see a certain edge state in myself. I was going to this edge and backing away, going to this edge and backing away. I realized I was getting frustrated with myself, yet I was beginning to blame the practice. The practice was not working, I told myself. Yet what was really happening was that I kept prioritizing my preferences as opposed to following what I truly, deeply wanted to be doing, which was challenging myself with the practice. And so that vigor and vitality were missing.

I had to stop fucking around. It was my twenty-fourth birthday. I said, *Okay, Koshin, what would it be like to make a ten-year vow of just showing up for practice all the time?* So I vowed to sit every day and to do every retreat. Every time that practice was offered at the Zen center, I would just go. I wouldn't wait for someone to invite me to participate deeper, but instead I would ask, "What's needed, and how can I help?"

In Zen we often suggest wholeheartedly trying something for thirty years and then, afterward, evaluating how it's going. I wasn't sure about thirty years yet, but ten years seemed like a good starting place. So I made this vow on my twenty-fourth birthday, and it shone a big spotlight on my preferences and how they were drawing me away from my true heart's desire.

Reflection

Is there a practice you've been hesitating to take on? Meditating every morning, connecting regularly with loved ones, skydiving, or something else? Instead of doing it or not doing it, vow to take on the practice for a time that feels palatable to you—maybe one month or three months. Tell yourself that you are just going to do it for that time period, and you'll evaluate later. Perhaps evaluate it in thirty years.

Holding off evaluating is a place of practice.

BRING YOUR FULL SELF

One of the many wonderful things about Zen training is that you are instructed to bring your full self to everything that you're doing. If you're cleaning, you're really cleaning. What is it like to wholeheartedly clean, to put everything into it?

When I was seventeen years old and practicing at Zen Mountain Monastery, I was in charge of cleaning a certain hallway. I had only this little hallway to clean. At first it seemed pretty easy; I swept the hallway and said to myself, "Uh, it looks pretty good," and then I was done. But then I looked closer, and I realized that right by the edge of the floor and the wall there was some grit that the broom wouldn't reach. And so I got down on my hands and knees and slowly made my way down the hallway, cleaning it, taking care of it. And for me it became an amazing thing to see how far that care could go.

I don't tend to think of myself as a person who gets into physical labor, yet in Zen training everything matters. And so how you slowly make your way and take care of the space that you're in for me was a wonderful way of really seeing both parts of me, the one that was caught up in this kind of laziness and said, "Just like sweep and go; it's fine," and the other that said, "Wait a second— that could go deeper." I think in some ways this wonderful little hallway was such an amazing place of learning.

Why Are You So Exhausted?

Some years later, I was working with a teacher on a five-week retreat, and I was introduced to the pathology of taking *too much* on. There is this part of me that I was still working with, which was *pleasing*, still trying to please, to be the good boy. I had the position of godo, the head of the meditation hall when the teacher was not present, and I was in charge of the whole retreat. I was also in charge of liturgy training, the overall well-being of the community, and registration. It was a lot. I was going nonstop, and I didn't know how to ask for help in a good way. And I got so exhausted just going, going, going. I felt like I was the one who needed to do all of that, but the lack of collaboration was its own kind of poverty of mind.

Somehow my body and mind careened through these five weeks, and it was a powerful retreat, but at the moment the retreat ended I felt so sick I could barely get out of bed. I felt so weak, so completely wiped out. I thought there was something terribly wrong with me. I went to Dr. Marty, my friend who was also my primary care physician, and he did some tests. What he said was, "So you know what's wrong with you?"

And I said, "What?"

And he said, "You're exhausted."

There was little nobility in what I had done, because I almost wiped myself out.

I had gotten way too tight, and I was dominated by old patterns of needing to prove myself, needing to take it all on. In the end, this wasn't about real service or real practice. It was about playing out my old stories.

Reflection

Do you find yourself exhausted? At times this may be a result of illness, not enough rest, or overwork, but often there is another cause. What is exhausting us may be something deeper than work. The next time you're engaged in an activity you find exhausting, pay attention. What is it that's draining your energy?

Nourishment is a place of practice.

RIDING THE OX, TAMING THE MIND

In the Zen tradition we have a teaching image of the spiritual path called the Ten Oxherding Pictures. The pictures have been painted by many different artists, usually with accompanying poetry. The first pictures in the series show the process of befriending the mind, taming it, and then learning to ride it—to be fully one with oneself, with one's attention and psychic vitality. Ultimately the ox is forgotten as the effort of coming back to oneself dissolves into effortlessly being who one is, and then forgetting even that. One is enabled to let go of all navel gazing and give freely to the world.

We'll discuss the later stages of the Ten Oxherding Pictures in the chapters to come, but here we will focus on the process of "taming" the mind, which I understand as a process of learning how to bring all of oneself to the present moment. Very often, without knowing it, without paying attention, our mind, our values, and all of the things that we want to create effort around go wandering off. And so then the mind feels like a feral creature.

Many years ago, I was working for a magazine, doing engaging work. It felt really meaningful. Then suddenly it stopped feeding me. The pleasure left. I was going through the motions, but something felt wrong. I went off to visit this little town called Turo in the south of Spain, because I knew I just needed time and space. I spent a month there in a writing retreat, which was an incredible privilege and returned a great joy inside me.

I was there alone with myself, I felt so sorrowful, I felt depleted. I felt that my oxygen had definitely gone somewhere else and I needed to go look for it. I set out to look for the footprints of the ox, to go into those grasses and to look for the tracks. What I found was that I was living at some distance from myself, from my heart. I needed to settle in, especially into my grief and pain, and act from there. I needed to bring more of myself to my life.

Many of us have this experience of feeling a lack of attunement, a wrongness in our effort and in our lives, and yet we stay where we are and accept it. We don't look for the ox; we focus only on the next thing we feel driven to do, the next fire to put out, the next distraction or self-medication. We can go on for years like that.

Meanwhile the ox is wandering off in the grasses, alone and lost. We need to seek it out. This may mean we need to actively move, to change in ways that may seem scary.

Reflection

Are there areas in your life where the ox wanders off? Where you feel disengaged, flat, struggling, off? Try taking some quiet time, being with that, and staying with it until you get an insight into what's wrong. Follow the tracks of the ox, with pen and paper if needed, and see if you can find what's blocking you from being fully present in that situation.

Finding your heart and mind is a place of practice.

And Then Keep Going

Once we make the effort and find the ox, we get this glimpse of how things could be different. Many of us have had that experience of glimpsing how we could be more integrated and feel more authentic. And that is, sadly, a place where many people stop. Many of us will get to that point, and then it seems too hard. We turn back, which is so heartbreaking. I think that that's one of the reasons why many people love Luke Skywalker or Bilbo Baggins. They are such shlemiels on a certain level, such annoying characters, whiny, fearful, foolish—just like us! Yet they keep going. It's hard to look for the ox, you know? How is it that we care too much for how hard change is? Yet, if we keep going, that's the source of all the adventures.

Integration

In my experience, real transformation takes time. It's about learning how to stay with the ox throughout the day, how to stay in touch with our highest understanding and our most authentic presence. That might mean, for instance, microdosing meditation. We can do one-minute sessions in the beginning, that's a start, and it can be a game changer.

It can be protective of our practice to have routines. I have a morning routine I follow almost every day: First, before I've even opened my eyes, I do my own version of a Jewish practice called the Modeh Ani. This entails calling to mind five things I am grateful for. I take care of our cats and then visit the small altars we have around the house, taking care of each one. I then exercise for about half an hour and afterward have breakfast and coffee. All of that, including breakfast, is a place of practice. After that's done, I bike to the Zen center to sit in meditation with the community. I find that when I do these things in the morning, mindfully and intentionally as practice, the day starts with clarity and energy. And it feels like whatever happens, happens, and I'm ready.

Reflection

How do you begin your day with intention and care? What would it be like to create a morning that actually sets you up for nourishment? What would be nourishing to you? Meditation? Movement? Gratitude practice? Delicious food?

Creating a morning ritual is a place of practice.

MICRODOSE MEDITATION

A friend of mine was having a lot of trouble meditating for a half hour a day, as their teacher recommended, so they talked to their teacher. The teacher listened and then said, "Why don't you try two hours?"

My friend set their mind to it, and though they couldn't find two one-hour periods, they meditated for ten minutes here, ten minutes there, twenty minutes here, five minutes there, and they found a way to make up the two hours throughout the day. When they had accomplished that for a while the teacher said, "Ok, now you can find your hour a day." At that point it seemed easy! They did that for many years, and it changed the quality of their mind.

We need to track down our ox and bring it back home, but then we need to spend time with it. It's shy, and it doesn't trust us, and maybe we don't trust it either. So we need to spend some time and care. Then we can begin the deep work of riding the ox, which is the work of untangling our attention and taking our seat in the world.

At some point in life the world's beauty becomes enough. You don't need to photograph, paint, or even remember it. It is enough.

—TONI MORRISON

CHAPTER 14

Attention Is a Place of Practice

When I was teaching a class recently, people were talking about the challenge of fully paying attention to other people and to the world around them. Some noted that it was easier to pay attention to some people more than others, and some felt that strong feelings made it hard to pay attention. Some shared visceral memories coming up in their body, which pulled their attention inward or into the past. Others' attention was impacted by pain or injuries they were wishing would go away. In the end, our attention is impacted by what we don't want to pay attention to, or by the pull of traumatic memories and strong feelings. As one of the participants stated, fully inhabiting our experience no matter what is happening undoes our inattention.

Why, though, do we need or want to pay attention? What's wrong with taking a ride on the monkey mind?

First we should note that in my understanding of the Soto Zen tradition, we don't cultivate attention so much in the way of focus or concentration; instead, we liberate our attention so that we can pay attention in a 360-degree kind of way. Why do we do this? Because the liberation of attention—the expansion of attention, you could say—liberates our wisdom, promotes mental flexibility, and, maybe most important, introduces us to the compassion in the whole of our life moment after moment. The monkey mind, too often, is on the run and missing most of what's actually happening.

There is a teaching I call the four facets of attention. It's a dynamic way of coming alive to how we are or are not paying attention. This can lead to great delight, even amid experiences that are painful. This may sound counterintuitive, but learning how to pay attention is learning how to ultimately bear witness to *what is* intimately, and to not turn away from it. So often we want to turn away. None of us have to practice that. We easily turn away from what's uncomfortable, even from what's delightful! For some of us, truthfully, pleasure and enjoyment can actually be uncomfortable, even threatening.

In this chapter we're going to explore different ways of paying attention and seeing that everything matters. This is resting in the nobility of learning how to ground ourselves in our own experience, in our bones, on the ground, so we can widen out and do something new—not be trapped in old patterns, in death.

I LOVE THE SEVEN SISTERS

There's an old story from China that I love in which seven sisters are hanging out, wondering how they wanted to engage the day.

One says, "Let's go see the gardens and plants."

One says, "Let's go to the charnel ground. We can watch the jackals and vultures eating the bodies!" The others all say, "Okay, let's go," and so they go. These sisters are open to all types of experience, to all the textures of life.

One of them says, "There are bodies here, but where do the people go?" This question provokes them, and they all wake up and have satori, transformative insights. Indra, the king of the gods, is so impressed that they could penetrate what so many fear to pay attention to that he offers them a boon. They say they don't want anything, but he presses them, and so they ask for "a shadowless tree and a valley that has no echo." He didn't understand this, so they sent him to the Buddha. The Buddha said, "They've woken up, so they don't need anything. They're free, they're complete."

This is the power of fearless attention. When we're willing to go toward what we conditionally fear, that's a road to freedom. Ultimately, the sisters realized there was nothing solid to be afraid of; the corpses were a process of constant change, empty of any persons or anything to fear. This kind of transformation reminds me of an amazing Sesame Street book, *The Monster at the End of This Book*. The book starts with lovable, furry old Grover in a panic. "There is a monster at the end of this book. So please do not turn the page." As you turn the pages, he pleads, begs, and tries to stop us from turning the pages. Each page he becomes more and more undone and exhausted. At last, we turn the page to the end of the book and who is there? Grover in his sweet blueness. We realize what we fear is often not tangible or actually there. It is our mind and its ideas that cause suffering and struggle.

Reflection

How do you move away from your fear?
Facing our fears is a place of practice.

FIRST FACET: OUR BODIES AND THE BODY OF THE WORLD

One day, I saw images of Haitian refugees at the border being whipped and brutalized by the US border patrol. It was so horrible, so dehumanizing, so terrifying. The images started to do something to my body, and I knew that something had been activated, something was surfacing, but I didn't know what.

Then, one of my contemplative care students was guiding a practice for us and inviting us to come into our bodies and remember a time when we felt unsafe. Suddenly this smell of the forest came into my nose, here in this loft in Chelsea in the middle of New York City. Then in my mind I heard screaming and the sounds of machines in the night. I realized they were the sounds of the four wheelers that had chased me when I was ten years old. Visceral memories came back, memories I hadn't recalled before, of just trying to get off the path and survive, and these people chasing me with guns and yelling, "Die Jew! Hunt the Jew!" I had been exploring the woods on the edge of my family's property, and the neighborhood teenagers had found me there. It became a nighttime activity for them, but a nightmare for me.

My heart started beating in my chest as I was sitting there on the cushion, and I remembered my uncle Victor, who escaped the Mauthausen concentration camp in 1942, talking about hiding when the Nazis were chasing him. All of this was in my body, and suddenly my body was in pain. I could remember running and jumping off the path through blackberry brambles, which clawed at my skin, and I got all cut up. I remembered trying to be completely still so those people in their four wheelers with their guns couldn't find me. Now, almost forty years later, reliving this memory, I began appreciating this attention to the body and what it can reveal.

As we came out of the meditation, I felt intense nausea. People were going around the circle, sharing what came up for them, and I was able to share what came up with me and actually experience myself still here, still feeling what I was feeling and learning how to regulate it. I felt my sit bones, and I found myself rocking back and forth, and thinking, *I'm here, I'm here*, and feeling my feet on the floor. This was about untangling time. I was not in danger at that moment; I was okay. With attention, somehow my mind and body came together forty years ago and sealed that memory. It felt like a miracle. Even writing this now is painful, yet loving attention and awareness is like a balm for what we carry in our bodies.

Tenderness

One of my students wrote to me that they were having a lot of visceral response to this recent example of cruelty in the news, and asked, "What value does the Dharma have in the face of that?" I felt such tenderness toward this person. The value of the teaching is that we can feel these visceral responses and find a refuge in ourselves through attention and untangling it, and what a gift it is to be able to receive in ourselves and in community.

In that moment of remembering I was sitting and practicing paying attention with others who were also learning that. That is a refuge we create together. In that context I was also able to give rise to a tenderness and a curiosity toward these people who were hunting a ten-year-old boy in the woods. What does it take to come to that? What has happened to these people that they would think it was a fun activity? They seemed joyful. I can still remember them laughing wildly—in a *Lord of the Flies* kind of way. All of this lives in our bodies. As V has written about, it's part of our bodies and part of the body of the world. As we learn to practice being in refuge in our own bodies, we can widen out to include the bodies of our communities and the body of the earth itself. This connectedness is perhaps only doable if we are non-separating from our own bodies as a starting place. When we are in denial of the pain in our own bodies, we are so much less likely to be able to make room for the pain of other people and beings in the world.

The specificity of our experience in our bodies—to feel our bodies, our breath, and our heartbeat, and to slow down and experience what we're actually experiencing—is so important. Some mornings I sit by the Hudson River, watching how the high tide swells it, and the waning moon sometimes is still visible and setting—the delight of that. When we can feel at rest, we can feel expansiveness, contraction, pleasure, and pain, and learn how to become our ocean. Like dear Leonard Cohen says, "If you don't become the ocean, you'll be seasick every day." We can feel the ocean in our bodies and not be caught in the swell and the heave, but find the expanse of it, the broad ocean, and find the great healing tenderness that is always available in the body when we pay attention.

Meditation

Sit in a comfortable position and tune in to the sensations of the body. See if you can feel the way the movement of the breath moves through the body like an ocean of sensation, first expanding the body, and then contracting it. Relax into this tidal movement of breath energy. Enjoy the flow of sensation, the electric tingling, the swell of movement.

Spend some time sitting in the flow of breath in the body like you were by the oceanside, watching the waves.

Experiencing the oneness of the body's rhythms with the rest of nature is a place of practice.

SECOND FACET: ENDURING FEELINGS LIKE CINDERELLA

I love the story of Cinderella. She might not seem like a paragon of spiritual strength, but think about it. She had to endure all of these challenges and difficult feelings. All she wanted to do was go to the ball. She wanted to participate in life and community ritual. She just wanted to dance. She had this great feeling of wanting to do that, but she wasn't allowed. She had a dress, and then it was torn up. She was weeping at the tree where her mother was buried, and out of her tears came her fairy godmother, and the fairy godmother gave her another beautiful dress. In such a short time she's feeling so many feelings. If she became one of those feelings, she would have been stuck. But no, she goes to the ball and meets the prince. How do we learn how to really inhabit what we're feeling right now, then the next thing, then the next, in attention to the feeling, not our stories about the feeling? Feelings will arise and pass away if we let them. It's our stories about them that tangle them up and tangle us up in the process.

What I find helpful is realizing that I don't know *this* feeling right now. I've never felt this feeling as it is right now. It's new. Then we're not in the story of the feeling; we're in the feeling itself. We're crying at our mother's grave; we're at the ball. Learning to simply experience it—oh, that's now!

I have found there are three steps in dealing with our feelings: having a beginner's mind about our own feelings and other people's feelings, bearing witness ("this is what this feeling feels like now)," and the loving action that flows out of that kind of attention.

THIRD FACET: RIDING THE OX OF MIND

My friend Dean is homeless, and he chooses to be homeless because he doesn't feel safe in the shelters. Sometimes when I see him, he's having a little conversation with himself, and I ask, "How's the conversation going?" And he says, "Hey, I'm just trying to find my mind." We can easily get lost. We all do that without being aware of it, maybe less aware than Dean. He knows when the ox has wandered off.

It is good for us to get curious about what our mental state is. How do we do that? Slowly. When we find the ox, when we catch it, this is so important. We need to be aware of this moment and hold it tenderly. Some people say, "It's so hard to collect my mind." I want to say, "So what? So what if it's hard?" Sometimes we care too much about how hard it is. "Hard" is a little overrated. Taking care of our attention is an art that can be practiced. Even if it takes years, it is well worth it.

In order to learn how to tame our ox, we need to show up with an attitude of willingness. It's a willingness to confront and love the mind, to do the work. We can understand that, okay, it's gone off again. Let's go out and find it. It's an attitude of friendliness too, of tenderness toward our ping-ponging mind. We need to be willing to find it and have a gentle attitude and patience. I heard Joseph Goldstein, the insight meditation teacher, once say that it's like we're climbing a circle. We have to put a lot of effort in to get to the top, and one day, we are at the bottom, and we go just a little way, and roll back, and a little way, and roll back, and we build up momentum, and it's not so hard. We learn how to be more skillful in our effort. We learn to be gentle with our straying and returning.

What Is This?

Many people are familiar with a rotund, laughing Buddha figure found in many Chinese restaurants and shops. Although often mistakenly thought to be the Buddha, it is actually a statue of Budai, a medieval Zen monk who was known for his humor, vagabond lifestyle, and kindness to children. After his death he came to be seen as a Santa Claus–like good luck figure that brings prosperity and happiness.

There is an interesting koan, or teaching story, about Budai befitting the joyous deity of dim sum and knick-knacks. In this koan it says that everywhere Budai traveled, he carried an old sack full of things with him, the same sack that, in other stories, is said to have contained gifts for children and the poor. In this story the sack contains his alms bowl and washing basin, his clogs, his food, and then the jarring, disorienting inclusion of roof tiles and bricks.

Budai would stop in a crowded place and take out these items and ask passersby to look at each one. Then he would demand, "What is this called?"

Of course, Budai knew what each one was called. What he was asking was, "What is this? Do you know what this is? Have you ever really looked?"

To really look at any object, we need to bring our full attention, our full being, all five senses. Then we can ask, "What is this?" Try it. If we ask, we will find that we don't know, and in that not-knowing is wonder and care.

Meditation

Right now take your seat comfortably and then look at an object near you. This can be something stationary, like a table, or something you can pick up, like a cup. Forget everything you know about it, and be aware of it with your full being and all five senses. What is it?

Allowing fullness is a place of practice.

Hello, It's Me

Hello again! Sometimes it's so sweet to say, "Hello again! I'm back. I was away." It's such an amazing thing when our mind state is collected. We can be together with our experience and with one another more intimately. We can feel when people have a collected mind state, because they're really where they are. I learned this from my grandma Mimi. She was that kind of person. My friends used to love to go visit her on their own. When you met her, she was completely there; her mind state was collected, and it was a melody you could join in to. She would remember everything about you. When we cultivate attention, it is not just a gift we are giving to ourselves. It is a gift we give to everyone around us. Our attention becomes a nourishing soil in which they can flourish.

Really paying attention reveals the ordinary as extraordinary.

Extraordinary Mind Is the Way

I was talking with a student the other day. They said, "You know, you often talk about how extraordinary everything is."

"Yes," I said.

"Well, what about how ordinary it is?"

I said, "Well, in my experience, when I'm really experiencing the ordinary, it is extraordinary."

Like many of us, I come from a lineage of people who didn't always learn how to make the effort to bring their actions and their intentions together. That was part of my inheritance: not really seeing things through. In my gut I wanted to be different because, as we all know, that doesn't feel good. When the lute was not too tight and not too loose, but engaged and vigorous, it felt amazing. I felt myself come alive. Riding the subway became a miracle. Of course, all that happened was that I was really there in my own normal life, but there wholeheartedly.

Often, we're not even in our experience. We're just kind of going along doing things, lost in the mind. We have things that we call "errands" as opposed to "Wow, I get to go to the grocery store, and I'm walking down an aisle with a million different vegetables that all have amazing shapes!" The antidote, which brings wonder, is showing up with our whole selves to what's right in front of us.

The Secret of Delight

The other day, one of my contemplative medicine fellows was talking about how she was practicing slowing down in her life. She was doing the laundry, which she never really thought about while she was doing it before. And suddenly she pulled up a seat, sat there, and thought, *Let me just do the laundry.* Sitting in front of the dryer, she found a new way of experiencing this seemingly mundane task as beautiful and amazing, watching her family's clothes spinning around. What a sweet practice.

Another person spoke to me recently about how amazing it was to watch their kid make breakfast for the first time. They had seen that kid make breakfast a million times, but they felt like they'd never seen their child actually go get a piece of bread out and spread peanut butter on it. Suddenly it struck them: This person didn't used to be able to do anything, and now look, they are feeding themself! Or this morning, I was noticing the black-eyed Susans someone had planted along the river. Wow! They were so perky, and blooming there, right there, was beautiful black-eyed Susan-ness. I was looking at what's happening in the sky, what's happening on the shore of New Jersey, and I saw a woman sitting on the side of the river and crying. Beauty and sorrow together.

From working in emergency rooms, I've learned a lot about suffering and delight. Many people come in with a loved one and regret how they had been fighting, or how they missed a chance to say goodbye. When we are attentive to this moment as it is, that is less likely to happen. Why? Because this moment is unique, impermanent, fragile, never to be repeated. One moment, one chance. Learning how to drop into life, as it is, is enriching and delightful. Learning how to slow down to now is the way to cultivate the delight of actually experiencing our sorrow and even the bizarreness and absurdity of the world. Really mingling with the people of the world means inviting all of the parts of our own selves in. We need to allow the tough parts, the textured parts, the parts that don't make sense, the parts that are ragged but yet blissful, because this is the delight of having a complex life, not a "complicated" life.

When I think of that woman crying that morning on the side of the river—it might sound strange to say—but just to take her in, even in her sorrow, offers a kind of delight. One can wish that she is relieved of her sorrow and yet still love her and delight in her in the midst of her expression of this very natural and inescapable part of being a human, just as she is. When we're receptive, we find the delight of the present moment, which is closely and intimately related to being aware of the impermanence of the present moment. Each moment is unique, will never happen again, and will pass.

FOURTH FACET: CARRYING THE TEACHING

The fourth facet of the jewel of attention is being mindful of the teachings that nourish us and keep us grounded. These teachings can at times act like a floating log on the waves of the ocean. They can be something that we can grab onto to prevent ourselves from going under.

In that spirit, every day we need to ask how we are creating the conditions that nourish our attention, that have our behavior match our values, and that bring us back to that source. I recommend that every day we read something nourishing or listen to an engaging talk to help us connect. One of my students carries around a spiritual teaching they find helpful: How do we build a life where there are mirrors and pictures in our life that nourish our attention to what we value?

Keeping Indra's Net in My Pocket

A mother came to the Zen center to speak with me one day, and we went into a private space. We sat down facing each other. All I knew going in was that her son had died by suicide. I was aware of my own tenderness toward her, and I was curious about how she was in general and how she was in her grief. She had found him and had to cut the rope down from the pipe in the basement, which is what she told me as we began. I felt it was not the moment to say anything at all, and yet I could give her my full attention.

She began sobbing and wailing, and her sweater became wet with tears and snot. I just sat there feeling the waves of her grief, just being with her. This went on for some time, maybe twenty or thirty minutes. She was grieving in this primal way. All I could give her was the facet of loving attention to *her* feelings, thoughts, and body—her wholeness. At a certain point she looked up at me, and I looked at her with a soft gaze, and she said, "This is a miracle."

"What is?" I asked.

"You're the first person to not tell me it's going to be okay, to tell me I'll get through it, to hand me a tissue. This is probably what brought me here today, to receive this."

The teaching that I had carried with me into that situation and that arose to show me how to hold her in my attention was the image of Indra's net from the *Avatamsaka Sutra*. Indra's net is a vast net of jewels, which is the whole universe, where every gem reflects every other gem. Nothing is separate. Remembering this teaching, I was able to see how her grief and her life were connected to every parent who has lost a child in terrible and difficult ways, and I was able to hold her in connection with all of those mothers.

The teaching I was carrying around, that we're all interconnected in ways that expand even beyond our normal sense of reality, is a support for how to express compassion through attention. The teaching of attention is everything. We often get busy trying to clean up when sometimes simply offering attention is what's most healing.

Reflection

How can you nourish attention to the teachings that have mattered most to you? Memorizing passages, carrying around wallet cards, making art, or placing helpful words around the house work for some people. Is there a way you can live with those teachings that bring you back to your deepest values?

Engaging with the teachings of our ancestors is a pl of practice.

If you are unable to find the truth right where you are, where else do you expect to find it?

—EIHEI DOGEN ZENJI

CHAPTER 15

Seated Meditation Is a Place of Practice

Some Zen books start off by talking a lot about seated meditation, which is called zazen in our tradition. In this book, I've done the opposite. As a result, at this point in the book, some readers might be wondering, *Isn't this a Zen book?* Perhaps! When are we going to talk about enlightenment? When are we going to talk about our awakened natures and deep meditation and enlightenment?

Well, it's kind of like doing yoga stretches before you meditate. Meditation doesn't stand on its own: The way you lead your life supports your meditation. And of course, the way you meditate supports your life. That's why so far we've been talking about how understanding and working with our suffering allows us to develop the path, and then discussing the eight aspects of the path. Technically only the last two stages of the path refer to meditation proper, and we've spent the last chapter and now this one focusing on it. The last chapter dealt with mindfulness, and this chapter deals with seated meditation, or zazen. Zazen is the eighth fold of the path.

UNDERSTANDING THE SELF

Dogen, my Soto Zen OG, has a famous essay called *Genjokoan*, which could be translated into English as "Fully Manifesting the Mystery of This Moment of Life." In the essay—which is quite mysterious itself—Dogen says that understanding the way of practice means understanding the self. He then says that to understand the self is to "forget the self."

In other words, we need to understand ourselves, and when we do that, we go beyond ourselves. Understanding ourselves means we need to start right here with our bodies, our suffering, our *meshugas*, our trauma. That's why we spent this much of this book studying how we get working with our suffering. However, one reason we are working with these giants of greed, hatred, resentment, delusion, and separateness in order to develop each of these steps of nobility is that they are needed so we can be still. As well as being valuable in themselves, of course, they are also what allow us to become truly present in meditation.

Why, though, are we sitting in zazen posture and becoming still at all?

Well, I don't know another thing that's more important than having a time each day of not doing and not thinking, to have the experience of not being pulled by all of the winds and the weather of life. Every morning, meditation gives us a chance to drop into the softness of our experience without following every thought-world that bubbles up. It's like climbing out of the river of the mind and sitting on the bank so that we can look at the flow of our thoughts, feelings, preferences, and opinions, of all of that, and learn to be with it in a very different way. And then we'll fall back into the river! We'll sink into the river and get into our feelings and our opinions and our blah, blah—and then climb out again. Doing this again and again creates the conditions for a life where our values are at the ground, because we are not so much at the mercy of our reactivity. Outside of how we usually react and who we usually think we are, it allows us to find our original strength, which is our true teacher.

Originally Perfect

In the beginning of another work by Dogen, the *Fukanzazengi* (Universal Guidelines for Zazen), he says, "the way is originally perfect and all pervading," by which he means that our true nature, which is the true nature expressing itself as everything, is already perfect. So why, then, do we need to practice? He writes:

The way is originally perfect and all-pervading. How could it be contingent on practice and realization?

The true vehicle is self-sufficient. What need is there for special effort?

Indeed, the whole body is free from dust. Who could believe in a means to brush it clean?

It is never apart from this very place; what is the use of traveling around to practice?

And yet, if there is a hairsbreadth deviation, it is like the gap between heaven and earth.

If the least like or dislike arises, the mind is lost in confusion.

Dogen is talking about what we root down into our practice, this perfection of our Buddha nature. *Buddha nature* means everyone has a space of freedom inside which can manifest as our capacity to wake up. It's so extraordinary, and it's not contingent on anything. You can't lose it. When we sit in meditation, we're dropping down into something that is not contingent on anything in our bodies or minds, or in the state of the world. It is not contingent on whether someone gives you a cookie, or someone in the grocery store moves their cart for you, or our parents loved us in a certain way, or any of the things that we get caught up in. It's this space of no cell phones, so to speak. Off the grid. No reception, and total receptivity.

GROUNDING

When we sit we are strongly grounded, which is a manifestation and an embodiment of our Buddha nature. We're just there, available, strong and planted. We're sitting at the side of the river, seeing the nature of life. We have a space where it's not just about us. We're not eclipsed by our preferences. We're not eclipsed by our field. We're not eclipsed by what we think, and we are in a relationship. That is what Dogen describes as "entering the Dharma gate of ease and joy." It's actually the joy that you can experience even with what's excruciating or even what is unbelievably gorgeous. As he says, though, if the smallest like or dislike captivates the mind, we can get lost in confusion. We fall back into the river. Our experience, most of the time, however, is not the fantasy of being a stoic and immovable being on the side of a river. We start thinking about what's for dinner or some message that you need to send. The practice is falling down seven times and getting up eight. So we're going to get drenched, again and again.

There's a great line in another essay of Dogen's that says, "You know, when you fall down to the ground, you get up by means of the ground." It comes from the story of Upagupta, who is the fifth ancestor in a line from Shakyamuni, and who was an untouchable, what is now called Dalit. We fall down, we fall in the river, and we have to use the river to get up. We have to get out of the river, but we have to be in relationship with the river and figure out how to get out. The return is so important, and the return is in the relationship we have to the river.

Mindful, Alert, and Ardent

When the Buddha taught meditation, he would always say, "When a person, mindful, ardent, and alert, having put aside greed and distress with regard to the world, sits down to meditate, then they should..." These are the attitudes that make meditation possible: mindfulness, ardency, alertness, and putting aside greed and distress with regard to the world. What does each one mean?

We have discussed being mindful—having our awareness in the present moment. Being ardent and alert means that we are keeping track of our ox and taking responsibility for ourselves. The key sentence here, though, is this: "having put aside greed and distress with regard to the world." When we're meditating, greed and distress with regard to the world are not the framework we meditate within. That means we don't judge our value as a person based on how our meditation goes. We leave behind the strategies of the ego and the categories of worldly success—even if it's the so-called spiritual world we're talking about.

When meditating on the body, we leave behind judging the body in terms of the world. We put aside thoughts and feelings like "Would the world think this body part is attractive or not? Is it healthy or not? Am I aging?" The same with feelings or thoughts that come up. We don't view them in terms of what they supposedly say about our worth as people, or what we imagine other people would say about them, or what we think they say about us. That's not the framework. We're not using greed and distress with regard to the world as the framework for what we're doing anymore.

Kodo Sawaki, one of the most important Soto Zen teachers in twentieth-century Japan, once said, in his typically provocative style, that when we do zazen we practice going back to our mother's womb. He also said zazen is "good for nothing." What he meant is that when we practice zazen, we put down all the losing and gaining, all the striving and struggle, all the trying to get or be anything. That's one of the reasons why zazen is so important. It gives us rest. It lets us experience ourselves apart from all that. Over time it also cultivates a ground where there are many more possibilities than those circumscribed by our normal greed and distress.

Samadhi

The eighth fold of the path is called zazen, which means collecting and bringing together the whole self. It's important to know that the process of that unification is not always pleasurable—sometimes it's excruciating. A student of mine recently told me that he had begun meditating, and all of these memories that he regretted, all of this pain over things he had done or been, came up. "I must be doing it wrong," he said to me. But for me, that's a crucial part of the process of samadhi, of gathering the self together.

So in our meditation, difficulty and discomfort will arise, guaranteed. It's going to be hard. It's going to be difficult, and to me, hitting that difficulty means it's going well. It reminds me of a powerful story of Osiris, the Egyptian god. When his brother was jealous of him, he chopped Osiris up into little bits and spread him out all over the world. Isis, his wife, in her grief, goes around the world and collects her beloved and pieces him back together. That's my image of somebody piecing themself back together. What has been torn asunder, maybe through history, conditioning, families, antisemitism, culture, racism, homophobia, transphobia—all of it—can be pieced back together and remembered, collected. It's important to know that sometimes this is going to be hard, and it might be painful, and there might be a lot of grief. Yet there is this powerful healing that can take place if we stay the course: *If we stay the course.* For one lifetime—at least! We need to allow all of ourselves to come up, to be gathered and to be present and to dissolve in the light of awareness without greed and distress with regard to the world. We allow ourselves to just be what we are, and we view ourselves in terms of zazen, which means we let thoughts and feelings arise and pass away without resistance or grasping. So let's talk about how to learn zazen.

ZAZEN

Posture is important for Zen meditation, whether it's done in a chair, lying down, on a cushion, or on a bench. We're going to go over the main points of the posture here so that we can understand the way it's the container in which we hold our heart and mind. As Dogen talks about it, what's key is how you hold all of it with what he called roshin, the grandmotherly mind we talked about. Some people can get intense and use posture like a weapon—which might be aimed at themselves or others. So before we even get into posture, let's remember that attitude, because the attitude in which we practice is so important.

The word *zazen* itself means "sitting Zen," and "Zen" comes from the Chinese word *ch'an*, which comes from the Sanskrit word *dhyana*, which means meditation. The Zen school is interested in how exactly we physically sit in meditation, but before we get into that, we need to say that the sitting is not essentially just about how you physically sit; it's about how you sit with fear and the ten thousand joys and the ten thousand sorrows. How do you learn, like the Buddha under the tree, to sit and not be blown away by the winds of life?

To begin, find a comfortable place to sit. Having a place in your home is helpful. Sometimes you don't have that space and have to improvise—sometimes you're in a hotel room or you live in a small space, and you have to get creative. Some friends of mine are incarcerated, and they have a tiny space. So whether you have tons of space or a little space, find your spot. The beauty of this practice is that you can do it anywhere.

Second, find a way to sit upright and comfortably. If you're sitting in a chair, sit upright under your own power if you can, unless you need back support, in which case sit against the back of the chair. Plant your feet on the ground. If you don't need the back support, sit at the front of the chair, so that your hips are tilted a little bit forward, which is energizing. There are also ways to sit with a little bench called a seiza bench, or you can sit on a cushion. Either way, have your knees on the ground to provide grounding. You want to create a strong base. It's also helpful, whatever your position, to rock a little bit back and forth, feeling your round sit bones and finding your center. Rotate your hips forward so that your lower spine curves a little bit. It can be helpful to stretch your arms behind you.

It's also helpful to open your shoulders by rolling them backward. We hold a lot of tension in our shoulders. Then put your hands in the hand position, or mudra, to use the fancy term, where your left hand lies in your right palm, and your thumbs lightly touch. Put your hands in your lap, close to your body, so your thumbs are approximately at a space two inches below your belly button. Having your thumbs near that area, you're creating a circle. You don't want to hold your hands too loose or too tight. If you allow your mind to wander too much, your hands will collapse.

Posture is a wonderful way to hold your heart and mind. Place your hands and then notice your breath in your hara, that place two inches below your belly button. And see, before you adjust further, what it is like to simply be with your breath and feel your lower belly expanding and contracting with your breath. Notice what happens with your mind as you do that.

Next, come back up through your spine. Imagine that the crown of your head is attached to the sky, so there's an uprightness there. Remember, though, that uprightness looks different for different bodies. You want to find a comfortable uprightness for you. Slightly tuck in your chin. And here's the tricky part: Lower your eyes to a forty-five-degree angle without tilting your head. Learn to keep your head upright while gazing down. In many forms of meditation, people close their eyes. In Zen meditation, we keep our eyes open and gaze down at a forty-five-degree angle.

Why do we do this? Well, the position we place our hands in is one often found on Buddha statues, and you may have noticed that Buddha statues all gaze downward in this same way. Taking this hand position and lowering our gaze is a way of saying that when we practice zazen, we embody Buddha. Before we discuss what we do—or don't do—while seated in zazen posture, let's explore what "embodying Buddha" means.

Embodying Buddha

As I see it, embodying Buddha means two things. The first thing is the Buddha nature we discussed earlier. We all have the capacity to wake up, and our deepest nature, which we touch in zazen, is already free and beyond all conditions. The second thing is that these aspects of our posture tell us that, as we say in my Soto tradition, practice itself is enlightenment. This means that taking up the posture of an awakened attitude in our lives is itself enlightenment. This practice-enlightenment deepens and deepens, but the way we practice is not to seek a "state of enlightenment" or to try to become "an enlightened being." For us, the approach is that simply showing up and practicing right now is the whole story. Whether we are enlightened or not is beside the point.

Posture and Breath

As you begin to sit, notice if you have put all the pieces of the posture together. Do you have a strong base? Can you feel your sit bones, the lengthening of your spine, the opening of your shoulders, the connection of your hands, and the uprightness of your head gazing down? Now notice your breath in your hara again, and feel if you need to adjust anything.

When you feel settled, it's time to pay attention to the breath at the hara. The foundational practice is counting the breath. On the inhalation, count one, and on the exhalation, count two, and so on. In theory, you go to ten, and then start at one again, like a circle. But the key part is that each time your mind wanders and you think, *What's for lunch? What's for dinner? Why didn't they email me?* then you come back to counting at one. I imagine it like going a little bit off-screen—you go too much this way or that way. You start following a thought, or going into some fantasy about something—then you just come back.

So if you count one and then you imagine, *How am I going to deal with that difficult person?*, you come back to one. Whatever it is, whatever distraction you're experiencing, no problem. Just come back to one. Come back to this moment. Other than noticing you've gone away, the most important thing is the attitude with which you catch yourself. Don't shame yourself, but rather learn to be loving with some vigor. Some people describe it as like bringing a puppy or a kitten back to where you want it to be. Just pick it up and bring it back gently and tenderly. Bring yourself back gently and tenderly.

The brain fires hundreds of thoughts a minute; it's just what it does. So having lots of thoughts is not a problem. We're learning how not to follow them, and yet to lovingly return with an acuity of attention with tenderness and love.

Let's try this. Together, we learn how to be free. I invite you to practice this on your own. You can start with as little as one minute. Find what's right for you, and begin.

Reflection

Take a moment now to pause. You may be sitting or standing or lying down or walking. Find your breath in your body. Where is it? In your neck? Shoulders? Chest? Solar plexus? Hara? Place your hands for a moment two inches below your belly button and feel the breath moving your hands. Allow the breath to move your hands for a few breaths. Pause and experience. What do you notice about your quality of mind? This is what we are cultivating in zazen: attention, love, and awareness.

Courageously beginning again and again is a place of practice.

LAYING THE FOUNDATION

For many years I practiced counting my breath as I described above. The thing is, counting your breath comes more from the tradition of concentration or focus practices, which has been taught from ancient times by different Buddhist schools, but which tends to be deemphasized in Zen. I think it's so valuable now, but for many years, I was sure that it was a terrible practice, because it didn't seem to me that it was the real white-hot core of Zen coolness. I thought, *Zen is about being with whatever arises, about embodying liberation, not about focusing on the breath! Not counting it, one, two, three, like a child!* Yet, when I practiced it, I found it incredibly helpful to count the breath to build steadiness, like building my own posture and getting my body used to actually having my shoulders open, which is a process, and learning to feel held in the ground.

For many years, I felt there were better things to do, more interesting things to do. Luckily, my teacher had a good sense of humor and waited until I was ready to get simple. Counting the breath and learning to be mindful, to focus, to bring yourself back gently, to root—these are all important, but these skills are not the be all and end all of Zen practice. They are a preparation for the core practice.

Shikantaza? What Is That?

The word sounds exotic, so it might come as a surprise to learn that it means "just sitting." And what it really means is being with things as they are. Once you have some facility with counting your breath, it's something you can try.

Shikantaza, just sitting, is a practice of open awareness. Dogen describes it as "the manifestation of ultimate reality":

Traps and snares can never reach it.
Once its heart is grasped, you are like a dragon gaining the
    water,
like a tiger taking to the mountains.

Some people think that meditation is kind of about chilling out, taking a pause, or spacing out. The way Dogen describes it, though, it is like "a dragon taking to the water." Zen is a tremendous energy and vitality and aliveness.

You are simply sitting, noticing when your mind has gone somewhere else, and returning. But here we are returning to open awareness and spaciousness. It's quite challenging. And I think that is why counting our breath for a good amount of time is so helpful, so that we can develop the confidence to stay with whatever's happening and have a strong anchor.

Bright Clarity

One of our Chinese ancestors, Hongzhi, was famous for his beautiful clarity in writing and embodied practice. About shikantaza he says,

> *Silent and serene,*
> *forgetting words,*
> *bright clarity*
> *appears before you.*

These are his instructions about how to sit shikantaza. The way that bright clarity appears before us is that when we're actually in our bodies, guess what? We're actually in our bodies. As I often tell my students—and myself—the great adventure is when you're walking down Twenty-Third Street and you're actually walking down Twenty-Third Street! Bright clarity appears before you.

You're awake, that's bright clarity. When you reflect it, you become vast. Where you embody it, you are spiritually uplifted. When you really see it in yourself, there's so much more space. When you're sitting in shikantaza and allowing yourself to drop in there, you reflect it, and then you widen out.

Shikantaza tends to be taught after counting the breath because of the importance of first learning how to root, root, root, so that once you're rooted, you can receive and reflect that vastness. I know it was definitely true for me that, in the beginning years of my practice, I felt that I wanted to run from shikantaza. It felt like too much. Maybe because it was almost insulting to my identity. In Zazen we put down our identities, our "greed and distress with regard to the world," and that can insult our self-obsessions and self-importance. I was so into my struggle and my suffering, my hurts. These were what brought me to Zen in the first place, and yet they were also what kept this vastness at bay. Eventually I was ready to face it, and what had seemed frightening became a field of play, a liberation.

Hongzhi says that where you embody shikantaza, you're spiritually uplifted. He's talking about moments where you embody it. Many people come to this practice and think that they're going to be like that model in the bathing suit on the cover of *Time* magazine about meditation: She looks great, but it looks like she's on vacation, and this practice is not about vacation. And yet Hongzhi, whom Dogen studied, is talking about this incredible spiritual uplift that actually happens in practice, over time, moment by moment.

Hongzhi then says,

spiritually solitary and shining,
inner illumination restores wonder.

To me, it's like talking about the healing that happens through zazen. "Spiritually solitary" is a feeling of containment within yourself, which, of course, is also to be contained in the world. Many people associate *solitary* with *lonely*, but what he's talking about here is the amazing capacity we each have to feel complete inside of ourselves, at ease and content. That inner illumination restores wonder. This is the phrase that has always inspired me when seeking someone to study with. What drew me to my teacher Dai En is that she completely embodies wonder.

So in sitting shikantaza, we have to remember that we're not trying to achieve anything, but we're trying to restore wonder. Practicing shikantaza is, in some ways, a simple practice. It's coming back to that vast and reflective awareness and simply being where you are. That's practice.

DAILY LIFE

The other day I decided to treat myself to an electric Citi Bike, which is a shared bike service we have in New York City. I got on the big blue bike and zoomed and zipped down to the Hudson River, but just as I got down this big hill the electric part of it conked out. Ironically, that makes it harder work than a normal bike; it's almost like pedaling through molasses. My first thought was *Shit!* And then I thought, *Okay, this is my place to practice. It's time to look into my preferences.* It doesn't matter whether I felt that the next docking station for this bike was really far away. I had to go; that was it. So I set off on the path along the Hudson river slowly, like through molasses. I had to stand up because pedaling was so tough. And so what I thought was going to be this quick little ride that usually takes me about twenty minutes ended up taking an hour and a half. Yet it was so amazing because what I found, in connecting to my hara and my belly, was amazing. I began to notice all the things around me. I started to notice that the Hudson River is tidal. Waves were coming up the river. V-shaped flocks of Canada geese were heading south. Because I was going so slowly, everything became really vivid. And I thought, *Okay, how do I take in where I am? Even though I would prefer to be zipping by now, who cares?*

This teaching of "who cares" is incredibly helpful. It can be a mantra. When we're in activity, and we can drop into where we are, who cares so much about your feelings and your preferences? In the end, I felt much more connected to the city and nature through this ride. I bike that path every day, and it was the "unfortunate event" that turned out to be an amazing experience. We need to remember over and over again to come into the body and to slow down. We need to say "who cares?" to some of the things that want us to rush or get caught up in thought or pulled away, and do the next thing that's right in front of us. That's our task.

In Zen we talk about having "big mind," not "small mind." Small mind is lost in reaction, but big mind attends to what happens in your personal life, your hopes and dreams and oatmeal, and at the same time appreciates that the sun is burning, that the rings of Saturn are turning in a mysterious way, that the gas giant Jupiter is floating out there, and Andromeda is moving closer to our galaxy and eventually will merge with the Milky Way. All of that is true. There's a saying from Padmasambhava, a master beloved in the Tibetan tradition, that expresses this understanding of a big mind: "Let your view be high as the sky, and your actions as fine as sand."

The other day, Chodo and I were waiting for a taxi to pick us up. As we were standing there, a person came by with these huge German shepherds. They came right in front of us, and one of the dogs took an enormous crap right in front of us, literally about eight inches from my shoe. You'd think they'd clean it up, maybe say something, but they kept walking. They didn't pick up the shit! They were clearly in their head, and even looked at the poop and looked at us, but then kept going with no clear awareness. At first, I was irate. Who does that? Then I realized that in many ways, when we're not in samadhi, not collected, we all do that. We all are living our life that way. We're walking our dog and not aware of how it's affecting other people. Zen practice is learning how to notice where the poop is and taking responsibility for it, and cleaning it up right away.

The important thing is not to stop questioning. Curiosity has its own reason for existence. One cannot help but be in awe when they contemplate the mysteries of eternity, of life, of the marvelous structure of reality. It is enough if one tries merely to comprehend a little of this mystery each day.

—ALBERT EINSTEIN

CHAPTER 16

Mystery Is a Place of Practice

We've walked the path together now. We've seen that untangling our perspective means shifting from "what has been done to me" to "what I am doing." With regard to others, it means finding a way to compassion through facing our own suffering. Untangling our intentions means asking the question, "How do I seek true nourishment that doesn't involve exploiting other people or doing them harm?" Untangling our speech means speaking with reflection and care, and not falling into the easy, habitual patterns of thoughtless or harmful speech.

Untangling our actions means getting in touch with our values and being clear about what those are. Untangling our work means learning from our work, and not separating it from our values. Untangling our life force sets our effort free—not too tight, not too loose, and sensitive to the actual effects of our actions.

Untangling our attention means cultivating the four facets of the jewel of attention—body, feelings, mind, and teachings. Untangling our seat is learning zazen, which is embodying Buddha both on and off the cushion. We've climbed a mountain of words—not too many, I hope, but the old masters might say definitely too many—and now we're at the top of a one-hundred-foot pole.

STEPPING OFF THE ONE-HUNDRED-FOOT POLE

An old Zen koan asks, "What do you do when you're on the top of a one-hundred-foot pole?" Imagine yourself there for a moment. You've put a lot of effort into reaching the top. You stand there, ruler of all you survey. In Mumon's *The Gateless Gate*, a classic of Zen koan literature, one master asks, "From the top of a pole one hundred feet high, how do you step forward?" Mumon tells us, "One sitting at the top of a pole, one hundred feet high, even if one has attained *it*, one has not yet been truly enlightened. One must step forward from the top of the pole one hundred feet high."

The point here is that holding on to attainments and understandings is not *it*; it's not what we're after. Even if we think we are doing fabulously—even if we think we have attained a new level of calm, or presence, or love, or self-acceptance, or clarity, or wherever we are seeking, we can't hold on to that. Everything changes. The path is not about attaining some kind of static state, or winning a Buddhific trophy—it's about how we approach each moment. How are you approaching this moment right now? As the Buddha said, in the *Bhaddekaratta Sutta*, when he was asked how to have an "auspicious day":

You shouldn't chase after the past
or place expectations on the future.

What is past
is left behind.
The future
is as yet unreached.
Whatever quality is present
you clearly see right there,
right there.
Not taken in,
unshaken,
that's how you develop the heart.

Stepping off the one-hundred-foot pole is like stepping into the void, stepping into the unknown, and the thing is, regardless of what we feel or think, that's always the reality. It's always true, each moment, that we're stepping into the unknown. We're always stepping off a one-hundred-foot pole, but most of the time we hide this from ourselves.

The final ox-herding picture is called *Entering the Marketplace*, and it shows a smiling character, carefree, clothes loose and open, hands spread wide. This is a state beyond samadhi, beyond collecting the self, beyond even sweet moments of zazen when we're letting everything go and resting in things just as they are. It shows the ox herder coming back to the marketplace with open hands and open heart—vulnerable, exposed, and joyful.

We all have times when we think we understand our lives, or we think we know how things are going to go. Maybe we're projecting the past into the present, or maybe we think our ducks are so lined up that we're feeling pretty darn confident we know how things are going to roll out. Either way, that's what we call hubris. The future won't necessarily reflect the past. I'm sure we can all remember times when we were *so sure* things were going to go a certain way. That certainty can set us up to react poorly when things don't go that way. When Ajahn Chah was told something, he would say, "It's not for sure." That's what he told his students to say to everything: "It's not for sure."

This might sound scary, but actually it's the Dharma gate of ease and joy that Dogen talks about again. It's available when we're grounded in ourselves, living in accord with our values, and no longer trying to be something. It's available when we are not relying on the next moment being a certain way, which is something we cultivate in zazen.

Being Curious

When Terry Dobson was studying aikido in Japan (he was one of the first Americans to do so), his teacher told him he needed to learn how to practice in the midst of everyday life, with people, with surprises. As a result, he started paying careful attention to the people around him and to his own reactions. One day he was on a train in Tokyo, and there was a really drunk guy on the train. He was big and being loud and aggressive. Terry was sitting there, feeling awkward, trying to imagine something he could do to address the guy's energy and turn it around. An elder who was sitting there schooled the drunk guy. Speaking gently and straightforwardly, the older gentleman said to the guy whose behavior was frightening people, "It seems like you've drunk a lot."

The younger guy said, "What are you talking about?"

"It seems that you're quite intoxicated," the older gentleman said gently.

The guy startled and said, "Yeah."

"Sometimes my wife and I really enjoy sake," the gentleman said. "Were you enjoying sake?"

And the guy said, "Yes, yes, yes. Yeah. I was."

"My wife and I, we like to have a little sake," the old man said. "We go outside and to a place in our backyard where we can sit on a little bench and look at our persimmon tree. Our persimmon tree is not doing so well, though, you know, maybe it has not quite gotten cold enough or warm enough or the soil is not so good. Persimmons are so delicious, though. Do you enjoy them with your wife or family sometimes after work?"

And the guy said, "I don't have a wife. She died, and I don't have anywhere to go."

"You sit down here," said the old man. And so the man sat down. They kept talking, and the old man listened, and all the people on the train started to relax.

The old man's strength was that he didn't assume things could only go one way, and he was willing to take a risk. He was being curious and open and clear.

WHAT ABOUT ENLIGHTENMENT?

You will find some Buddhist books that take the idea of enlightenment seriously and argue that one can progress through certain well-defined stages of increasing freedom. Finally, one can go totally beyond delusion and suffering. Other Buddhist books pooh-pooh the idea of a final stage and argue that we will never go beyond confusion and human limitations. They suggest that spiritual awakening actually requires letting go of such perfectionist paradigms. I want to suggest a middle way.

Most of us cannot honestly say that we know what the furthest reaches of freedom are. More importantly, though, it doesn't matter. The practice is not about reaching for a final attainment, an absolute, a trophy—a divine cookie, if you will, or a Buddha badge. It's about showing up to this moment in a posture of practice. When Dogen says that practice *is* enlightenment, that is what he means and perhaps all we need to know. Will it ever end? What happens next? That's the mystery. Why try to solve it? It's the beginning of a great adventure of a life of continuous practice. Let's go together.

APPENDIX 1

Resources

Samyutta Nikaya: www.accesstoinsight.org/tipitaka/sn/index.html.

Perle Besserman and Manfred B. Steger, *Zen Radicals, Rebels, and Reformers*.

Antonio Machado, *Border of a Dream: Selected Poems of Antonio Machado*.

Vaca Sutta: A Statement, www.accesstoinsight.org/tipitaka/an/an05/an05.198.than.html.

"Old Man's Advice to Youth: 'Never Lose a Holy Curiosity,'" *Life*, May 2, 1955, p. 64.

The New York Zen Center for Contemplative Care (www.zencare.org) is an educational nonprofit providing contemplative education and care and Zen practice. It is open to everyone.

The National Suicide Prevention Lifeline (1-800-273-8255) and the Crisis Text Line (text HOME to 741741) offer free twenty-four-hour support.

The Trevor Project supports the challenges that young LGBTQ people face. Twenty-four-hour live support is available: call 866-488-7386 or text START to 678678.

The National Domestic Violence Hotline is available at 800-799-7233.

Further Reflection for Untangling with the Four Noble Truths

For the past several years, I have been contemplating these teachings as a guide for our daily life. I encourage you to use these questions as a place to return to for reflection and digging deeper.

1. Everything is tangled in a tangle.
   What is the story you are telling yourself that causes you to suffer and become tangled?

2. The giants are a place of practice.
   How do you suffer with the giant of greed?
   How do you suffer with the giant of resentment?
   How do you suffer with the giant of delusion?
   How are they alive in you today?

3. Pivoting is a place of practice.
   What supports you in change?
   What are the aspects of your life that nourish change?

How can you care for those seeds that support your growth today?

4. Perspective is a place of practice.
   How can you see clearly how you create the tangle and the causes of it?
   What would it be like to not feed the tangle?

5. Thoughts are a place of practice.
   How can you experiment with new ways of working with your habitual thoughts today?

6. Speech is a place of practice.
   How do you talk to yourself and others?
   What is underneath your words?
   How can you attend to your breath while speaking and explore new ways of speaking to yourself and others from the ground of your ethics and values?

7. Action is a place of practice.
   How do your actions allow you to maintain your struggles?
   Which actions allow you to embody something new?
   How can you foster wholehearted action?

8. Work is a place of practice.
   How can you shift how you embody your values in your attitude about work?
   How can you allow work to be a place to explore gratitude and care?

9. Effort is a place of practice.

   How do you explore if you need to soften your effort or if you need to tighten your effort to change?

   How can you reach out for support to nourish the right attunement of energy?

10. Attention is a place of practice.

    How can you open your eyes in a new way today?

    How can you listen with your whole body?

11. Seated meditation is a place of practice.

    How can you allow yourself to nourish stillness in zazen?

    How can you deepen your connection with others and a teacher to both support your meditation and the meditation of others?

12. Mystery is a place of practice.

    How can you allow the confusion, disorientation and mystery to be a place of rest and curiosity?

    How can you cultivate a life that welcomes mystery?

Acknowledgments

First, I am grateful to you, dear reader. I wrote this imagining offering you something of use.

I would not be here without the generations of ancestors in the Soto Zen lineage who dedicated their lives to the practice of awakening for and with others. Each day I am nourished by our beloved New York Zen Center for Contemplative Care sangha. Deep thanks to Sherry Salman for being a steady guide for our deep work. Blessings to Sensei Dai En Friedman for her steady unconditional love. Deep gratitude to Genyu Kojima Roshi for his trust, care, and guidance. Each month I am supported in such important ways by my Dharma friends Gyokei Yokoyama, Joan Amaral, Ayo Yetunde, Ben Connelly, and Chodo. Twice a year, I have the honor of teaching and learning from them and these beautiful teachers: Chimyo Atkinson, Chozen Bays, Norman Fischer, Issho Fujita, Konjin Godwin, Paul Haller, Taiga Ito, Koyu Mori, Shinzan Palma, Sato Ryoki, Shishin Wick, and Yuko Wakayama Yamada, all of whom remind me of the beauty of our unique expressions of love and practice. Your dedication and continuous practice of loving action inspires me.

So delighted to know Emma Varvaloucas, who is a friend and collaborator and, along with Jim Mintz, supported the forming of

240 Acknowledgments

the imaging for this book. Thank you to my friend Jay Michaelson, who connected me to Matthew Zachary Gindin, my developmental editor. Together we forged true companionship and friendship and love. So grateful to my friend Sebene Selassie for connecting me with her agent Anna Knutson Geller, who became a champion of the Dharma in this book and believed in its mission and found it a beautiful home. The door was opened by Nana K. Twumasi, my fabulous editor; from the first moment we met, I was connected and felt welcomed and encouraged. To the fabulous team at Hachette, especially Alexandra Hernandez, Kimberly Lew, Natalie Bautista, and Bob Castillo.

Readers are tender people. Thank you to Dan Harris for his generosity, humor, and straight feedback and friendship; Susa Talon for her tenderness and loving attention and friendship; dearest Martin Moran for his careful reading and generosity and love. Celeste Lecesne, bless you for your expansive reading and reflecting back a wider vision of the work and which inspired major rethinking and major love. Feedback from each of you changed me and the work itself.

Thank you to the Wisdom Publications team, particularly Daniel Aitkin, Kestrel Montague, and Laura Cunningham for your years of friendship and midwifing *Awake at the Bedside* and *Wholehearted* together—which brought me here.

Service is a place of practice. I continue to learn such a great deal about generosity, integrity, and ethics through my board service at the New York Zen Center for Contemplative Care, Soto Zen Buddhist Association, and Barre Center for Buddhist Studies. It is an honor to grow and serve the larger mission of the Buddhadharma together.

Thank you to my daddy-o, Richard Ellison, who continues to learn and learn with me about love and showing up. His emotional and thoughtful support nourish me. To my momma, Kenya Paley, for giving me life and a model for serving and caring deeply about social goodness. Just a few years ago I learned that my grandpa George and grandma Mimi were my godparents. Grandpa George, your love of Jewish people, the world, and me allowed me to expand and widen out. Grandma Mimi, I miss you so. You continue to accompany me each day and encourage me to keep widening out the circles of compassion and love. Both of your unique and specific loves for me changed and forged me, and you both continue to teach me about caring for the world and community.

Chodo. Chodo. Chodo. Never would I have imagined what real husbanding was. With you I continue to learn how to ground, how to get more tender, and about the wide breadth of love. Bless you. I love you to Andromeda and back.

About the Author

Sensei Koshin Paley Ellison, MFA, LMSW, DMIN, is an author, Zen teacher, and Jungian psychotherapist. Koshin co-founded the New York Zen Center for Contemplative Care, a nonprofit center offering contemplative approaches to care through education, care partnering, and Zen practice. Koshin is a renowned thought leader in contemplative medicine; his pioneering work has been featured in the *New York Times* and on PBS and *CBS Sunday Morning*, among other media outlets.